Council on Learning

Education and the World View

Change Magazine Press

This book is an adaptation of a special May/June 1980 *Change* Magazine issue on global issues and the educational response. This volume and several companion publications are part of the Education and the World View project sponsored by the Council on Learning. Major funding for this effort was provided by the National Endowment for the Humanities and the Exxon Education Foundation.

Contents

About the Authors

CYRUS R. VANCE is a partner in Simpson, Thacher & Bartlett of New York City. He has served as U.S. Secretary of the Army, Deputy Secretary of Defense, U.S. negotiator at the Paris Peace Conference on Vietnam, and most recently as U.S. Secretary of State.

GEORGE W. BONHAM is the executive director of the Council on Learning and editor-at-large of *Change* Magazine.

SHIRLEY M. HUFSTEDLER, a former U. S. Court of Appeals judge, was the first Secretary of Education of the United States. She has been a trustee of the Aspen Institute for Humanistic Studies, Occidental College, and the California Institute of Technology.

THOMAS S. BARROWS is a research scientist at the Educational Testing Service. He has had overall responsibility for the Global Understanding Survey and developed the affective portion of the survey.

STEPHEN F. KLEIN is a senior examiner at the Educational Testing Service. He was responsible for development of the knowledge section of the Global Understanding Survey and previously directed the *New York Times* survey of American history.

JOHN L. D. CLARK is a senior examiner at the Educational Testing Service. He developed the foreign language section of the Global Understanding Survey. He has been chairman of the Northeast Conference on the Teaching of Foreign Languages.

HARLAN CLEVELAND is director of the Hubert H. Humphrey Institute of Public Affairs at the University of Minnesota. Until recently he headed the international affairs program of the Aspen Institute. A political scientist and public executive, he has served as Assistant Secretary of State, U.S. Ambassador to NATO, and president of the University of Hawaii.

WESLEY W. POSVAR is chancellor of the University of Pittsburgh. A graduate of West Point and a Rhodes Scholar, he participated in the Berlin Airlift and has served in many internationally oriented positions in and out of the academy.

FREDERICK RUDOLPH, Mark Hopkins Professor of History at Williams College, is author of *The American College and University: A History* and *Curriculum: A History of the American Undergraduate Course of Study*. He is one of three executive editors of *Change*.

S. FREDERICK STARR, vice president for academic affairs at Tulane University, was secretary of the Kennan Institute for Advanced Russian Studies of the Woodrow Wilson International Center for Scholars in Washington, D.C. He has also taught history at Princeton.

RALPH H. SMUCKLER, dean of international studies and programs at Michigan State University, has written widely on development assistance abroad, institution building, and education for development.

DAVID J. DELL is director of program development at the Council for Intercultural Studies and Programs. A specialist in Indic languages and cultures, he is also a research associate at Columbia University.

THE COUNCIL ON LEARNING
TASK FORCE ON EDUCATION & THE WORLD VIEW

Foreword

Whatever one's view of the world and America's place in it, there can be little disagreement that the last decade or two have dramatically challenged virtually every traditional assumption about our global circumstances. The rapidity and pervasiveness with which global events now affect our national and private lives leave little doubt that we are in the midst of significant new transitions in our national future.

Regardless of what the future holds in regard to these global uncertainties, there is a fundamental question of how such fresh national circumstances should reflect on our educational content. The issue cannot be overlooked by anyone who understands the necessity in a democratic society for wide public understanding of the country's national and international policies .

This book on educating for a world view is one of a series of publications to have emerged from a two-year exercise by the Council on Learning. It was principally supported by the National Endowment for the Humanities to encourage fundamental changes in learning content to reflect new world realities. A distinguished panel of Americans, a roster of which appears opposite, helped formulate the major agendas for this project. We are grateful for their creative support and counsel as we are to the National Endowment for the Humanities, the Exxon Education Foundation, and the Department of Education whose support of various segments made this project possible.

Robert Black
Project Director
Education and the World View

Chapter 1

The End of Innocence

Cyrus R. Vance

The world, as we have known it through much of this century, is rapidly changing. We can either work to shape this world in a wise and effective manner or become paralyzed by its kaleidoscopic changes. To be our own masters we must understand our global environment for what it really is: a world in more rapid flux, a world in which neither the United States nor any other nation holds a preponderance of power or a monopoly of wisdom, a world in which events can no longer be ordered by those nations who hold the bulk of economic, political, and military power. Since our schools and universities are the fundamental institutions through which we gain an understanding of the world, it must be upon them that we rely to illuminate our perceptions of the world as it really is.

Widely divergent views are held on many foreign policy issues, and they should be argued out in informed public debate. But such debates are useless if those views are based on assumptions that are outworn or the product of seeing things that never were through rose-colored glasses.

To see the contemporary world as an age in which the United States still holds most of the ace cards is a serious misreading of global circumstances. That view severely overestimates our power and responsibility for ill and it underestimates our ability to do good in the world. And it is wrong for us to assume that the United States has the power to order the world according to our preference, and fallacious to think that we could dominate the Soviet Union. It is also naive for us to believe, as some do, that the Soviets would be willing to assume a military position that is inferior to our own. Such notions are antiquated and demonstrably obsolete.

But all of this does not mean that we are weak or lack the power to shape our future. The realization that we are not omnipotent should not make us feel that we have lost our power or the will to use it. If we appreciate the extraordinary strengths we have, if we understand the nature of the changes taking place in the world, and if we act effectively to help shape different kinds of change, we have every reason to be confident about our future.

This leads me to the importance of our educational institutions and the role that they must play. The special obligations which the country's major institutions must now bear—particularly education and the public media—are abundantly clear. For it is in our schools and in our universities that each generation first learns of its world. The complexities of this uncertain age thus impose special responsibilities on them to help create a deeper comprehension of global issues that will make the years to follow more understandable to the body politic.

In a new report to the Club of Rome on the role of learning in determining our global agendas, the authors say that "inadequate contemporary learning contributes to the deteriorating human condition and a widening of the human gap.... Learning processes are lagging appallingly behind and are leaving both individuals and societies unprepared to meet the challenges posed by global issues."[*]

It would be difficult to disagree that what we learn about the fundamental issues underlying the present turmoil in the world will help us, both individually and as a nation, to develop coherent responses, even to what appear at times to be incoherent foreign events. How education is to respond to these new worldwide realities is of course for educators to say. But it has been my experience that few foreign policy issues are easily subsumed under a single field such as history, economics, sociology, political science, or anthropology. More typically they combine all of these and more. To view and analyze the Iranian hostage situation within the single intellectual terrain of a political scientist or an historian is not likely to bring us an adequate understanding and analysis of this most complex problem.

There is no longer a purely geopolitical view or a purely international economic view. Our position around the world is often the consequence of many circumstances and events, small and large, obvious and obscure. No single analysis is now likely to suffice.

Despite the difficulties posed by almost endless complexities, I can-

---

[*] James W. Botkin, Mahdi Elmandjra, and Mircea Maliztza, *No Limits to Learning: Bridging the Human Gap*, Oxford and New York: Pergamon Press, 1979, page 9.

not think of anything more important to ask of our schools and colleges than to address themselves to that most essential educational goal: to provide young Americans with a more sophisticated understanding of our universal condition. Education is a search for truth, and while truth in searching for understanding of other peoples and other national aspirations is frequently relative and inadequate, that effort must be made, whatever the human impediments of mind and heart.

We also need to clear our minds as we set the nation's long-range goals for the decade ahead. To this end we must avoid certain fallacies of thought so that we can develop a coherent set of goals that will enable us to steer a wise course over the long term. The first fallacy is thinking that we continue to live in a bipolar world, and that a single grand superpower design will achieve our national objectives. The world has become so pluralistic that such a single-track strategy obviously no longer works. A second fallacy is our general fear of negotiation, since Americans often believe that they will inevitably get the short end of the stick. But without achieving a fair bargain there can be no hope for a more permanent understanding among nations.

A third fallacy is to believe that there exists an incompatibility between our foreign policy objectives and our fundamental values— such as human rights. Within the bounds of practicality and national security needs, our ideals and our foreign interests do coincide. We have a stake in the stability of nations who can freely express their own hopes and human aspirations. A final fallacy is the widespread assumption that military power can solve most non-military problems. Any review of our recent national experience shows the inadequacy of that analysis. And we must always remember that schools and universities are the institutions where these fallacies and these myths must be addressed, so that the minds of the young are free to address the realities of the world that we and they will live in.

I believe that most Americans now recognize that in unsettled times such as those we now face, each of us has a responsibility to be clear about how we would deal with the world as we find it. Most Americans now recognize that we alone cannot dictate world events. This recognition, however, is not a sign of the United States' decline. It is a sign of growing American maturity in a complex world.

We will be stronger today if we recognize the realities of our times. A deeper understanding of these, together with an equally clear understanding that we remain the most powerful of nations, should make every American as staunchly optimistic about our nation's future as we have always been.

We must go forward into a new era of mature American leadership —based on strength, not belligerence; on steadiness, not impulse; on confidence, not fear. We have every reason to be confident. For 200 years we have prospered by welcoming and adapting to change, not by resisting it. We have understood at home and abroad that stability is not the *status quo*. That can only come through human progress.

Chapter 2

Education and the World View

George W. Bonham

The French poet Paul Valery once remarked that "the trouble with our times is that the future is not what it used to be." Were he alive today, he might lament that the future has also become well-nigh incomprehensible.

For me as a nonacademic, the internal academic discussions over the future of international education seem to lie in the shadow of the vastly more urgent imperatives of our continued national existence. We are dealing here with a puzzle of extraordinary magnitude: For all of America's long years as a world power, for all of its engagements—peaceful or otherwise—in virtually every nook and cranny of this globe, we now witness an entirely new stage in world development; and yet we hardly see it at all. We fail dismally to unhook ourselves from ideologies that are no longer consonant with the new motor forces of world events. We stubbornly cling to easy dichotomies—East-West; Capitalist-Communist; the haves and have nots —and we fail to see the true world of vast new multiplications of cultural forces in which the old ideologies are not only incorrect, but keeping them may lead to disastrous consequences.

We are like Don Quixote, as if, for the first time out of our cultural village, we see the outside with new and unaccustomed eyes. What is particularly puzzling about our apparent failure to separate our long ingrown perceptions and new world circumstance is the fact that this is a nation that has been to the moon and back. Have we learned so little from our Apollo missions into space? From hundreds of miles up, all global perspectives can be understood in one stunning moment of recognition: that the world is but a speck in the universe, and it is fragile, and it does not come in two halves.

To put the matter more directly: We live in a world that is increasingly anarchical, increasingly unpredictable, and increasingly a world not of American choosing or of America's imagination. We may now find ourselves at one of the great disjunctures of our national history. Event after event brings home the fact that we understand each less and less and clamor more and more for simple answers. The role that education must play in the years ahead is inexorable and plain to see.

The world has unalterably changed, and so must American education.

What is at stake here is a major sea change in the way we must perceive global events, in the relationships of nations, and in understanding new strategic consequences. This is a world which by the end of this century may see 90 percent of its population living in the so-called Third World. Unless the major institutions in this very rich country —and especially education, the communications media, and our public agencies—resist the easy answers and prepare us for a world of vastly diffused power, our bad public arguments in regard to international order must inevitably become bad public decisions. And bad public decisions can only lead to foreign adventures the consequences of which no one can foresee.

If there is to be any convincing appeal to American education to respond more imaginatively to the incoherences of our time, it can no longer be made on the grounds of missionary spirits or encoded in the service of one-worlders or "the universe of man." The world is now a vastly splintered universe. This new diffusion of ethnic, cultural, and nationalist power leads to new ways of understanding a world that is less and less made in our own image or indeed in that of the Soviet Union, our prime antagonist. If we are to meet this new challenge to education, it cannot merely be a paean to multicultural diversity, or to peace at any price. The new peace studies that are now cropping up on our campuses are, of course, welcome developments, but they should not exclude courses on national security matters or, to put it more clearly, on "war studies." Whatever the educational offering, it should not be mounted in the service of a single ideology, but should represent a substantive reading of a globe where virtually every answer now promises to be exceedingly complex and beyond the social imagination of most of us.

Our old ways of thinking are made all the more difficult by our current frustrations as a global power with what most of us still presume to be our consummate global clout. We seem helpless in influencing events in Nicaragua or Iran or Afghanistan, but have not yet developed the necessary global imagination to be comfortable with other choices and other alternatives. These old ways of thinking die slowly with nations, as they do with individuals. We only seem sensitive to the unpleasant facets of an interdependent world, a circumstance unprecedented in the American experience. It is difficult for the mind to adapt to new ways of thinking, and especially to adapt to new systems of which we may be but a small part. In this regard our political leaders face a particularly difficult period in dealing with global disorder. Whoever is now intimately involved in foreign policy, their po-

litical fortunes are likely to plummet, if not for their inherent inept-
ness, then for the unpredictable reaction of public opinion. Much of it
still prefers to send the Marines to Tripoli rather than give up the Panama Canal.

Thus, except in the broadest possible intellectual terms, adoption of
a new "world view" by our political leadership is not likely to lead to
political success. One heard neither of the two Presidential candidates
in the past campaign comment on the Brandt Commission's recent recommendations to begin shifting world wealth from the haves to the
have nots, nor are they likely to avow in public that not all threats to
our national survival issue from the Kremlin. Former Senator Frank
Church, and ex-chairman of the Senate Foreign Relations Committee,
found himself in a tough reelection battle in Idaho, and his strategy
was to emphasize the local issues. "If you are asking whether I can win
this election on foreign policy issues," the senator admitted recently,
"the answer is probably no. There is a general feeling that things aren't
going well abroad and we can't do anything about it."

There are other indications that our frustrations abroad are leading
not to growing public sophistication in these issues, but quite the opposite. A recent Potomac Associates poll shows that there has been a
consistent decline in internationalist sentiments between 1964 and
1972, followed by an even sharper decline between 1972 and 1974,
and it has not turned around. Better-educated and higher-status
Americans, the study shows, do pay more attention to world events
and show a higher level of interest in foreign policy, and are also generally more supportive of international commitments. Poorer and less
well-educated Americans know and care little about foreign affairs,
and they see few links between global issues and their daily lives.

It is clear, therefore, that a growing interest in foreign affairs by
educated Americans does not necessarily connote a clearer understanding of a world in the process of transition. The television networks have recently recognized this growing interest in international
developments, and now fill the gap with additional television news
programs and documentaries. Unhappily, the endless complexities of
foreign cultures and foreign politics are not topics that easily lend
themselves to the camera lens or to the twenty-eight-minute television
segment.

There is now a clear need for a new world order, but the very
thought of that prospect runs cold shivers down the spines of most of
us. The reshaping of that world order is occurring before our eyes, but
only a firmer understanding of the likely shape of things to come will
give us any sense of control over our destinies. A firmer educational

footing of this global understanding is the first essential step in developing prudent political sensitivities. In dealing with other cultures, it will pay us to listen more carefully. We have usually asked others to listen to us. To listen carefully to viewpoints other than our own is, alas, not generally taught well in our universities.

I have placed international understanding into the larger political framework in order for us to better understand the true educational challenges. When we launched this public project on Education and the World View, we were under no illusions that this exercise would be easy, whether seen from our national political experience or from the vantage point of the educational record of achievement in this area. While I cannot speak for our task force of distinguished members, I doubt that any of us considered the challenge as open to instant solutions or as likely to receive the enthusiastic plaudits of the nation's 3,200 colleges and universities. The geopolitical complexities are real enough, but so are present-day academic organizations.

The world is divided into problems; the universities, however, are divided into departments. Enhancing the global dimensions of higher education, especially if they are to be more fully integrated into epistemological substructures, in fact faces hurdles of considerable magnitude. When added against the new fiscal conservatism imposed on academic institutions and the general public frustration with foreign affairs, one senses how difficult and challenging these prospects are likely to be.

It may well be asked why our colleges and universities should take on this very large task of moving "forward to basics," to use Harlan Cleveland's felicitous term, when in fact there is so obviously no particular public demand for it. The kernel to that answer lies essentially in the role that higher education wishes to play in the annals of contemporary affairs. We cannot say that any general resolve by educators to come educationally to grips with the new realities around the world will add to campus endowments or indeed win them points in the opinion polls. Still and all, it is the colleges and universities that still have available a certain flexibility of intellectual choice, to serve the interests of future generations as well as serving the lessons of the past.

When all is said and done, it comes down to a matter of faith: Will the universities themselves keep control of their essential purposes? No one dealt with this central question better than Walter Lippman did many years ago: "We must ask ourselves," he asked, "why, in the quest of a good life in a good society, we now turn to the universities rather than, let us say, to the churches or the government. We do that because the behavior of man depends ultimately on what he believes to be true about the nature of man and the universe in which he lives, to be true about man's destiny in historical time, to be true about the nature of good and evil and how to know the difference, to be true about the way to ascertain and to recognize the truth and to distinguish it from error.

"In other times and in other places, the possessors and guardians of true knowledge have been held to be the appointed spokesmen of a universal and indisputable tradition and of divine revelation. In the Western society to which we belong the traditional guardians and spokesmen of true knowledge have in varying degrees lost or renounced their titles to speak with complete authority. The hierarchy of priests, the dynasties of rulers, the courtiers, the civil servants, and the commissars have to give way...and there is left as the court of last resort when the truth is at issue 'the ancient and universal company of scholars.' "

It may not be overstating matters to say that the ancient order is now in a growing state of dissolution. Our academic institutions could become instrumental in providing a more pervasive understanding of the new order that is replacing the old. The campuses will be, in Lippman's words, our "courts of last resort."

Academic institutions, by the nature of their central purposes of pursuing the larger truths, cannot by that definition be parochial institutions. They must tilt toward the larger moments of human history. Despite the contradictory currents that now flow through our political life in regard to foreign affairs and the vexing uncertainties of our global existence, despite our forlorn record of international education, there is also cause for optimism. My first real recognition that matters might be turned around in invigorating higher education with wider global perspectives came to me two years ago after having written an editorial about the sorry state of international education, particularly when seen against growing international complexities. The editorial, called "The Future Forsaken," prompted more mail than I received that year on any other subject. It was clear that many people sensed that the time had come to move again in exploring educational alternatives.

The Council on Learning's Education and the World View project is a carefully defined public project of two years' duration to encourage serious curricular reconsiderations in our schools and colleges in view of the new realities of the world. This project follows hard on the heels of the President's recent Commission on Foreign Language and International Studies, a report which since its November 1979 release has

mustered a well-deserved national debate over many of these important issues. Other significant documents on international education
added to this new wave of concern: a recent Carnegie Council volume
by Barbara Burn; a major report on language study by a Modern Language Association panel; and a still more recent special issue of the
Annals of the American Academy of Political and Social Science. All
of these works distinguish themselves in my view for their realistic and
imaginative approaches to a complex set of issues. Unlike typical writ-
ings on this subject, all of these public documents are remarkably free
of the usual rhetoric and imprecations.

There remains little doubt that many of the campuses are beginning
to do their homework in exploring ways to broaden students' intellectual horizons. The whole occupation again with the consideration of
core curricula and alternative patterns of course offerings represents
an open invitation to reconsider once more the proposition that an undergraduate experience should expose students to other cultures and
to new world circumstances. Despite the general need of campuses to
batten down their hatches in this academic recession, there now seems
a growing sense of will to explore at least what is possible even under
constrained circumstances.

Lest one is too quickly overcome by unaccustomed euphoria, it
must also be said that those in international education begin with certain inherent handicaps. These should be bluntly stated. My first basic
premise is that the traditional organization of scholarly life is ill suited
to deal with global issues that inevitably cross every conceivable arena
of knowledge. Interdisciplinary work can be one answer, but much of
it suffers from inferior quality and sometimes makes up the intellectual playgrounds of dilettantes. Logic would tell us to begin with each
primary discipline, especially those clustering across the humanities.
This would require a thorough review by the best people in each field:
of curricula, syllabi, textbooks, catalog offerings. It should be a
systematic scanning of one's scholarly map, of what is transmitted to
one's students, of *what* is taught, and *how*. I doubt that the key disciplines look at problems and solutions in that way; indeed, few of them
would consider pedagogy, teaching habits, and national priorities as
essential businesses of disciplinary life. The monastic comes into immediate conflict with what must ultimately be seen as a secular crisis.
One ought not be overly optimistic of having these two worlds meet
on some common ground.

A further inherent difficulty of international education is a matter
that is taken up elsewhere in these pages. This is the fact that much of
what now is programmatically identified as international education is

essentially weaned on federal moneys. When these dry up, so, it seems, does much of international education. This roller coaster quality of funding, referred to by Frederick Starr in this volume, contributes to the tenuous character of international studies, and does little to serve the nation's interests of providing the young with a more profound view of international life. I find it not a little evocative that so much of what federal support there is for international studies falls under the rubric of "national defense." As if this is the best political argument for improved global visions. There are clearly more long-term interests involved here, and we ought to be sufficiently mature as a people to deem such investments appropriate for the long view.

For quite logical reasons, the role of foreign languages in enhancing an understanding of other cultures reflects one of the central debates over international education. I for one take the pragmatic view that while a thorough comprehension of at least one foreign language by each of our 11 million undergraduates would be a splendid addition to cultural understanding, we are not likely to get such competence in more than one-tenth of the student population. I would much rather put sparse moneys to providing comprehensive opportunities within the main curriculum, and in the better institutions begin to insist on solid foreign language work as well. This is a much-disputed subject, with obviously contrary views that deserve equal consideration.

One of the less discussed facets of the declining role of foreign languages, however, is not the instructional side but the academic hierarchy itself. Only in relatively few colleges and universities do foreign language departments find themselves in the campus mainstream. In all too many places, from personal observations, foreign language teachers regard themselves, next to the librarians, as the new pariahs of the academic workplace. Possibly, in some cases, philological eccentricities contribute to their political predicaments. Nonetheless, in the majority of cases, foreign language teachers have fallen victim to a certain intellectual arrogance of their colleagues in the key disciplines, who perhaps feel the study of foreign languages to be a less pure way to make a living.

I shall mention one other disturbing academic habit that seems to me inimical to the further development of international education. Because of its historic stepchild relationship to the rest of the academic enterprise, widespread divisiveness within the international field seriously handicaps any possibility of a widening role. Battles over academic turf and sparse funding have over the tough years created serious fissures in the international education community. I have always thought that I should be less concerned about the legitimate interests of the research universities for area study and interdisciplinary centers, since they well know how to argue their interests and enjoy a certain political clout. Even the foreign language teachers are ably represented within the Modern Language Association, and their voices are now clearly heard and understood. But who speaks for the lowly undergraduate? College presidents, faced by the impossible tasks of enhancing college incomes while reducing expenses, are hardly able to make special pleas for international education funding when the center enterprise is in danger of eclipse. It is simply too much to ask. And yet, the integrationist approach to globalizing the undergraduate learning experience should be one of the first orders of education's business. But, ill defined and relatively ill represented, that approach is also the least likely to find its way home in government and funding circles, let alone on the campuses themselves.

I have dwelled on these endemic distortions as a way of describing the central purposes of our Education and the World View project. This was also much on the mind of the National Endowment for the Humanities when it funded this project against, I might say, considerable political odds, much of which stemmed from the nuances I just mentioned. There is something to be said for those who are attracted to the tough propositions. I simply cannot believe that adding a thousand more area specialists to doctoral programs is going to resolve the larger issue of an enlightened and educated new generation that will spend much of its adult life in the next century. To meet the goals of the latter, it would be hard to imagine anything more central to the purposes of this country and its educational institutions.

A national task force of outstanding Americans helped guide this public project. They represent a wide variety of academic institutions, federal and state government agencies, concerned leaders in the corporate community, and the media. Through committees, many of them are actively involved themselves in details of the project designed to eventually convince those yet to be convinced that we must substantially modify what undergraduates learn about their world.

A further understanding of these issues was helped along by a number of national meetings. Six books are part of the result of our efforts. Of special note are a major book on curricular strategies, authored by Humphrey Tonkin of the University of Pennsylvania, and a descriptive book of workable international programs at 50 campuses around the country. All of this has taken the collaboration of a wide variety of professionals as well as the public at large. To have lasting effect, we need to include leading scholars, the scholarly and academic associations, academic leaders and teachers on our 3,200 campuses, and the resolve and support of nonacademic bodies such as state and federal agencies, foundations, alumni groups, and others concerned with the future of American education. The ETS study of college freshmen and seniors represents in a way a monumental study of great complexity, and is likely to be a fascinating road map for campus and curriculum planners for years to come.

In the final analysis, the degree to which our schools and campuses will adapt to a world of dramatically new form will depend on the resolve of a sufficient number of wise people to clearly see these new imperatives. This Education and the World View project is a very public and catalytic venture. Let it not be said in retrospect that it came ahead of its time. That time is here and now.

Chapter 3

A World in Transition

Shirley M. Hufstedler

It is hard for foreigners visiting our country to believe that we are still debating the necessity of enlarging the international component of our general school and college curricula. To be sure, America's national sense of self has been largely informed by our particular history; by our relative self-sufficiency; by our boundless frontiers; by vast oceans protecting our eastern and western frontiers; and by our emergence at the end of the Second World War as the leading and most powerful nation in the world.

But the world has changed profoundly since 1945. Today the effects of an event on one side of the world are likely to ripple all the way around the globe. Calculations of national sovereignty are routinely affected by the interests and needs of over 160 other nations. There is no longer a country on the face of this shrunken planet that can go it alone. Kenneth Boulding said it well when he conjectured that "if the human race is to survive, it will have to change its ways of thinking more in the next 25 years than it has in the last 25,000."

In an age of oil shortages, massive population movements, and fluctuating currencies, it is increasingly difficult to separate domestic from global issues. Our civic concerns can now be rarely seen in purely local or national terms, and few non-American events are any longer in fact extraneous to our lives. Our mass media reflect these new complexities fairly well; but the interrelatedness of global and national events is still only marginally reflected in what young Americans are learning in their schools and colleges. As a recent *Change* Magazine editorial warned, "America's young face a set of new national and international circumstances about which they have only the faintest of notions. They are, globally speaking, blind, deaf, and dumb; and thus handicapped, they will soon determine the future directions of this nation." The growing disparity between the realities of an interdependent world and the relative parochialism of our schools and colleges cannot help damaging the nation's capacity to decide its wisest future course.

Intelligent public choices will require that our citizens be attuned to the great forces that are shaping the modern world. We are going to have to learn to look at international conduct and national survival in new and unaccustomed ways. We deal today with a world that is increasingly fragmented. Rather than approaching a "planetary culture," as some had predicted, we are awash in new political subunits brought about by nationalist fervor, tribalism, religious movements, and thrusts toward cultural and ethnic self-determination. Strong and at times unpredictable forces—of both centrifugal and centripetal kinds—are creating new problems and instabilities throughout the world.

We have also entered an era of transnational corporations—of new business and economic realities, the implications of which we are only just beginning to understand. As Peter Drucker has pointed out, the traditional territorial political unit no longer corresponds to an enterprise that seeks economy of world scale. All of us, and especially the next generation, need to understand far better how these trends will affect our lives.

Unstructured violence is now a fact of international life. The Iranian hostage crisis is but one example of the frustrations and complexities of international violence that run deep in our domestic concerns. Aside from the resolution of the Iranian issues, all of us need to learn a good deal about the winds of change that are blowing with such force across the globe. Public comprehension of what is at stake is all the more necessary, I fear, since unstructured violence appears more likely to increase than to abate in the years ahead.

We cannot hope to understand such twentieth-century dilemmas with nineteenth-century curricula. Our educators are going to have to take a hard new look at what they are teaching—and not teaching —about the world. Until very recently American education has been almost exclusively concerned with our own national experience. To take care of foreign cultures and foreign history, one threw in, however reluctantly, a course on Western civilization and perhaps one or another European language. Even this was too often poorly taught and left unrelated either to a particular culture or to anything else being taught at the time.

This artificial isolation and intellectual compartmentalization hardly fits today's world. We must somehow contrive to equip our students with sufficient empathy to understand and deal realistically with other cultures. If we do not, as Clark Kerr recently pointed out, "we will never overcome the typically American feeling that if we can only make clear where we sit, all reasonable people everywhere will agree with the correctness of our policy stance instead of 'stubbornly' holding to their own. Only by sitting in another's place can we learn that there are real and legitimate conflicts of values and interests among the peoples of the world, as well as a common core of humanity and concern about our mutual planetary home."

Clark Kerr's words reflect, I believe, a very broad consensus. We may not all agree on how we should get there, but we do know where we want to go. The question now is, how do we begin our journey? And what can the new Department of Education do to help along the way? I am under no illusion that the formation of a department has transported us instantly—or even quickly—to our destination. This journey will have to be taken freely by thousands of school districts, colleges, and universities all across the country. There can be no coercion from Washington. But I do believe that we can take steps at the national level that will set our feet on the proper path. We have already taken some actions that demonstrate our strong commitment to international education:

- Despite the need to reduce federal spending, we have obtained a 50 percent hike in appropriations for the department's international studies programs.
- We have upgraded the organizational unit that has responsibility for international education. This unit is being led by a deputy assistant secretary who reports directly to Albert Bowker, the distinguished assistant secretary for postsecondary education.
- We have authorized the organization of a small unit within the immediate office of the secretary to coordinate policy toward international organizations and to insure productive participation in bilateral agreements. This unit is being supervised by Deputy Undersecretary Margaret McKenna.

These initiatives are a beginning, nothing more; but they do indicate the measure of our commitment to international education, and of our intention to develop increasingly efficient and useful activities within the department. Even as the department takes an increasingly active role, however, the nation will continue to depend heavily on private initiative. Our educational system, fortunately, is more easily influenced from outside than dominated from above. That is why I am particularly pleased that the Council on Learning has taken on the task of encouraging colleges and universities to reconsider their educational responsibilities in this whole complex field. I am confident that the Council's leadership will help trigger renewed interest and commitment on the part of this nation's academic institutions.

There can be no question but that we need the kind of fresh thinking that will come out of this initiative. What is needed is a conscious effort to overhaul our educational experience: to take a fresh look at existing curricular offerings, at textbooks, at syllabi, at the quality of language teaching, and, indeed, at the capacities of teachers. This is an effort that must be done on 3,200 campuses, in 3,200 variations. Such sea changes in the way we teach and learn about the world will not be effected by massive infusions of moneys, but only by massive infusions of fresh intellectual vigor and commitment.

I heartily concur with the President's Commission on Foreign Language and International Studies' conclusion that "on a planet shrunken by the technology of instant communications, there is little safety behind a Maginot Line of scientific and scholarly isolationism. In our schools and colleges as well as in our public media of communications, and in the everyday dialogue within our communities, the situation cries out for a better comprehension of our place and our potential in a world that, though it still expects much from America, no longer takes American supremacy for granted. Nor do this country's children and youths, and it is for them, and their understanding of their own society, that an international perspective is indispensable."

For the nation's colleges and universities, nothing on their agendas is more important than a serious reconsideration of their educative responsibilities to their nation and their world.

Chapter 4

What College Seniors Know About Their World

Thomas S. Barrows, John L. D. Clark, Stephen F. Klein

Students graduating from American colleges today live in a world whose people and institutions are increasingly interdependent. Are these educated citizens prepared to understand the interactions of nations in an interdependent world? Do they apprehend world problems from a universal and multidisciplinary point of view, and can they appreciate the immense complexity of both the causes and effects of these issues? Do they perceive the extent to which individual lives, including their own, are affected by global or international conditions, and do historical perspectives guide their understanding?

Several years ago the Educational Testing Service conducted a major survey of fourth, eighth, and twelfth graders' knowledge and attitudes about other peoples and other nations. (Lewis W. Pike and Thomas S. Barrows, *Other Nations, Other Peoples: A Survey of Student Interests, Knowledge, and Perceptions*, HEW Publication No. 78-19004, Washington, D.C., GPO 1979.) The results proved generally disconcerting to educators and social observers alike. The majority of the students had a surprisingly limited understanding of other countries.

But would college students understand their world any better, given their exposure to more advanced training and education? Until recently, answers to this question have been based largely on hearsay and anecdotal information. But now we have some solid answers.

As a significant part of its Education and the World View project, the Council on Learning asked the Educational Testing Service to develop and conduct a national assessment of what college students actually know and perceive about global relationships and to measure their comprehension of current global complexities. This ambitious student survey, funded by the Office (now Department) of Education and supported by the National Endowment for the Humanities, was conducted by ETS earlier this year. It is based upon a carefully chosen representative sample of over 3,000 undergraduates across the country. Some 185 institutions of learning assisted. This important and in many respects precedent-setting student assessment was guided by a

special panel of outstanding scholars (see box) whose counsel and assistance began in the early design stage and will continue through the
final interpretation of results. In this first reporting out, we shall only
deal with college seniors.

Assessment Committee

ROBERT F. DERNBERGER
Professor of Economics
University of Michigan

A. DAVID HILL, JR.
Professor of Geography
University of Colorado

WILLIAM J. McGUIRE
Professor of Psychology
Yale University

WILLIAM H. McNEILL
Robert A. Milliken Distinguished
    Service Professor of History
University of Chicago

RICHARD C. SNYDER
Director Emeritus, Mershon Center
The Ohio State University

JUDITH V. TORNEY-PURTA
Professor of Psychology
University of Illinois at Chicago Circle

G. RICHARD TUCKER
Director
Center for Applied Linguistics

IMMANUEL WALLERSTEIN
Professor of Sociology
State University of New York at
    Binghamton

Partial results for the 1,000 seniors are now ready.* Following are
some of the most significant findings:

- Seniors achieved a mean score of 50.5 questions correct
out of 101 on the test, showing a considerable lack of
knowledge on topics felt important by the assessment committee.

- Significant score differences occurred among seniors in
different fields of study. History majors scored highest
(59.3), while education majors—the teachers of tomorrow
—scored lowest (39.8).

- Patterns of response to specific test questions indicated
that important misconceptions existed. Even able students
had misconceptions about the following:

    ✔ The degree to which the dependence of the United
    States on foreign oil increased during the 1970s and
    the vulnerability of the United States economy to in-
    creases in the price of oil or decreases in the supply.
    ✔ The membership of OPEC and the reasons it can
    raise oil prices.
    ✔ The causes of inadequate nutrition as a global
    problem.

---

*The complete report on the 1980 national assessment of college students by the Educational
Testing Service is available from Change Magazine Press (271 North Avenue, New Rochelle,
N.Y. 10801, $10.95). The full report details the complete findings for all students tested on
the over 450 variables covered in this national survey.

✓ The United States' record on signing human rights treaties adopted by the United Nations and the major accomplishment of the Helsinki Accords.

✓ The comparative world membership of Islam and Christianity and the countries in which Islam predominates or has a significant minority.

✓ The difficulties connected with either national self-sufficiency or dependency in a world of interdependent nations.

✓ The historical origins of the Western sovereign territorial state and the modern state system and the emergence of nationalist movements as significant political forces in European history.

✓ The patterns of world birth and death rates today.

✓ The pattern of the world's past and possible future consumption of fossil fuels.

✓ The reasons for the lack of substantial progress toward world peace during the twentieth century.

✓ The main purpose of the recently completed multilateral trade negotiations, and the demands of representatives of developing countries in the North-South talks.

• The relative standing of seniors on the test was most directly related to their scores on parts of the test that dealt with arts and culture, war and armaments, race and ethnicity, relations among states, and international monetary and trade arrangements—topics usually encountered in traditional fields of undergraduate study. Topics such as environment, population, energy, human rights, health, and food, which fit less readily into the established framework of the academic disciplines, produced patterns of performance that were less similar to the pattern for the total test.

• Almost 90 percent of the seniors reported in the language self-assessment section that they had "learned or studied" a foreign language. However, despite the large number reporting foreign language study, useful levels of proficiency are being attained by very few. For example, only about one third reported that they could quite easily "order a simple meal in a restaurant," and only 11 percent felt themselves able to "tell what I plan to be doing five years from now," using appropriate future tenses.

• Foreign language ability is unrelated to scores on the knowledge test, although the possibility of a threshold effect attributable to extensive language study remains to be investigated. Affect, by contrast, is moderately associated with both language proficiency and knowledge.

• Fewer than one in twelve seniors had participated in formal programs abroad (only one in twenty had been in a year-long program), although almost 65 percent reported having been in other countries (mostly Canada, Mexico, and those of Western Europe).

• Taken together, the survey results indicate that global understanding is not a single entity but must be thought of as having three principal components: knowledge, affect, and language. The knowledge factor is defined primarily by scores on the knowledge test as well as by the habit of acquiring international news through newspaper reading. Affect is defined largely by several attitudinal measures that are predominantly, but not exclusively, political in nature. The language factor is defined by foreign language abilities, learning experiences, and attitudes toward foreign language study.

• Although television viewing was reported as the main source of information on current affairs, frequency of TV news viewing was not related to knowledge. Newspaper reading was.

The Survey Measures
The table below provides a seven-category description of survey measures. The original survey design called for developing measures of four presumed components of global understanding: (1) background, experience, and interests; (2) foreign language training, ability, and attitudes; (3) knowledge; and (4) affect (attitudes, interests, values, and so forth). In its final form, the survey included over 450 variables, far too many to list here. The seven categories given constitute only one of many possible maps that may be of some help to the reader.

One section of the survey was designed to provide a comprehensive assessment of elements of a student's background that might influence the development of global understanding. Sociocultural perspective appeared to be significant, so the survey asked about the respondent's ethnicity, country of birth, and socioeconomic status. Questions on student and parental political preferences and attitudes were also included. Because intellectual ability is consistently associated with most academic achievement, the student's scholastic achievement was queried through self-report of high school grades, national test scores, and college grade point averages.

Because formal and informal educational experiences were believed to affect global understanding, respondents were asked about their years of high school study in traditional course areas as well as the number of college courses they took in 19 subject areas. They were also asked about the extent to which they discussed world problems or issues in their high school and college classes and how much they

---

SURVEY MEASURES

General Background
Age
Sex
Ethnicity
Country of birth
Parents' education
Parents' political party preference
Parents' political attitudes
   (left/right)

Scholastic Ability
High school grades
SAT/ACT scores
College GPA

Educational Experiences
High school academic experiences
College academic experiences
Extracurricular activities
College major
Educational objective
Foreign travel

Interests
Amount and type of television viewing (news, current events, specials about foreign countries)
Reading habits (newspapers, magazines, general reading)
Main source of current events information
Political party preference
Political attitudes (left/right)

Affect
Perceptions of eight world issues:
   Environmental Pollution
Denial of Basic Human Rights
Unemployment
Intergroup Conflict
Depletion of Natural Resources
Inflation
Malnutrition and Inadequate
   Health Care
International Conflict and War
Five Likert-type scales:
   Chauvinism
   World Government
   Cooperation
   War
   Human Rights
One self-report scale:
   Concern
Twelve error-choice items

Language Background
Native language
Parents' native language(s)
Amount of formal foreign language study
Types of informal foreign language acquisition
Designation of "most proficient foreign language"
   (MPFL)
Self-assessment of MPFL:
   Speaking ability
   Listening comprehension
   Reading proficiency
Attitudes toward foreign language learning

Knowledge
101 multiple-choice test items

---

thought experiences outside the classroom contributed to their global awareness. Students were asked about curriculum-related informal educational experiences, including extracurricular activities, overseas travel, and summer- and year-abroad programs. They were asked to indicate their college majors and educational goals. The ways in which students acquire information seemed likely to be related to global understanding, so a series of questions probed media viewing, listening, and reading habits.

Four measures developed through extensive pretesting provided a more specific focus on the affective domain of students' global understanding. The first, which concerned perceptions of world issues, asked students to rate eight issues on several descriptive scales, such as whether the issue was important, whether the issue would become more of a problem or less over the next 20 years, and so on. The second asked students to agree or disagree with 32 statements indicative of attitudes toward chauvinism, world government, cooperation, war, and human rights.

The third technique consisted of a self-report scale labeled "Concern." Students were asked to respond true or false to 10 potentially self-descriptive statements such as "I make an effort to meet people from other cultures" or "I find the customs of foreigners difficult to understand." The scale was designed to measure interest, empathy, and reasonable freedom from ethnocentrism.

The fourth attitude measure was labeled "error-choice." These test questions were designed to appear to be factual and were embedded among the multiple-choice knowledge questions in the survey. The error-choice questions presented answer options that required students to overestimate or underestimate the severity or frequency of problems connected with such things as malnutrition, world nuclear stockpiles, or developing nations' GNPs.

Because laymen and language teachers generally believe that language study has a positive effect in developing an understanding of other peoples and cultures, the students' foreign-language background, level of proficiency, and attitudes toward language study were queried as an important part of the survey. Since it was not feasible to administer direct tests of each respondent's language skills, self-assessment scales in speaking, listening, and reading were developed. In a preliminary study, the self-assessments of a number of undergraduate French and Spanish language students were correlated with the results of standardized direct tests—the *MLA-Cooperative Foreign Language Tests* for listening and reading and the well-known Foreign Service Institute face-to-face interviewing technique as a measure of speaking proficiency. The resultant correlations were sufficiently high to permit use of these self-assessment scales as measures of language proficiency in the survey. Pretested questions on interest in and motivation for foreign language study, perceived personal and practical value in acquiring language competence, and related issues resulted in a scale of 15 questions measuring "Language Attitudes."

For the knowledge test, the assessment committee decided that of two approaches—traditional international relations and area studies or global issues transcending nations and regions—the issues approach was preferable. This approach required a global scope and included multiple dimensions (economic, political, social, and so on). Particularly important was the opportunity to trace ramifications of issues across time, space, and social institutions. Thus 101 questions clustered around 13 topics were eventually chosen. The topics and number of questions on each were as follows: environment (5), food (7), health (6), international monetary and trade arrangements (9), population (10), energy (9), race and ethnicity (8), human rights (6), war and armaments (8), arts and culture (8), religious issues (6), relations among states (10), distributions of natural characteristics (4). Also included were five questions from a previous precollegiate survey.

The final collection of questions incorporated the work of experts in a number of disciplines, writers, and editors. They were originally written by the assessment committee, by faculty at Eisenhower College (one of the few institutions of higher learning that has a core curriculum in world studies), by experts in various disciplines at numerous colleges and universities, and by several small groups of subject-matter experts and project staff assembled by ETS for workshops. The questions were rewritten, revised, and edited by the assessment committee, project staff, and ETS test-development specialists.

Selected Survey Results

The median age of the seniors in the survey sample was 21.9 years and the mode was 21 years. The youngest senior was 18 and the oldest was 52. Ninety-four percent of the seniors were born in the United States. Of the 6 percent not born in this country, 85 percent indicated that they consider themselves permanent residents of the United States. The remaining 0.9 percent of the respondents were foreign students and other visitors to the U.S.

Seniors reported greater exposure to world problems and issues in high school than in college classes (see box). There are many plausible

SENIORS' CLASS DISCUSSIONS OF WORLD PROBLEMS		
	High School	College
At least once a day	19.6%	18.4%
Once or twice a week	54.2	39.2
Less than once a week	23.5	29.9
Never	2.8	12.5

explanations for this: High school classes are generally smaller and more open to discussions; they tend to be less restricted by disciplinary confines; and they are probably more frequently taught from a current events perspective.

Of those seniors who indicated that they had "learned or studied a modern foreign language" (89.9 percent of the total), about one third reported that they had acquired a "survival" level of skill in the language (for example, understanding slow and deliberately simplified speech, asking directions on the street, reading storefront signs). However, a much smaller proportion rated themselves as having a working proficiency in situations that would commonly be encountered in travel, study, or employment abroad or in employment in foreign firms in the United States. For example, only 7 percent said they could read a popular novel without using a dictionary, and barely 5 percent considered themselves easily able to "state and support with examples and reasons a position on a controversial topic."

The survey contained several questions designed to show how students acquire information on world affairs (see boxes). More seniors

SENIORS' USE OF MEDIA

Watch TV or read paper	National TV news	Newspaper	Radio news	Listen to radio
Daily	25.1%	35.9%	33.7%	More than once a day
5-6 x a week	14.3	9.8	23.5	Once a day
3-4 x a week	27.7	23.4	25.4	Several times a week
1-2 x a week	18.8	19.9	8.4	About once a week
Less than once a week	14.0	11.0	9.0	Less than once a week

SECTIONS OF NEWSPAPERS READ BY SENIORS

National news articles	84.3%
Local news articles	76.7
International news articles	69.7
State news articles	61.4
Entertainment	61.1
Sports	44.0
Home/Living	22.1
Financial/Business	18.8

reported reading newspapers daily than watching television news; yet in response to another question almost 45 percent reported that they considered television news their main source of current affairs information, followed by newspapers (28 percent), radio (20.4 percent), and magazines (7.3 percent). When asked which 4 of 16 articles represented by fictitious headlines they would choose to read, they chose on the average one article with an international headline (see box).

SENIORS' SELECTION OF NEWS ARTICLES

(*international articles)

53.1%	PRESIDENT CONSIDERING WAGE-PRICE FREEZE
49.5	TEAM OF NEW YORK SURGEONS REATTACH MAN'S SEVERED LEG
46.7	ASTROPHYSICIST'S FINDINGS CAST LIGHT ON 'BLACK HOLES'
39.6	INDIAN GOVERNMENT STEPS UP VOLUNTARY STERIL-IZATION CAMPAIGN*
38.1	NEW COMPUTER TERMINAL 'TALKS' AND 'LISTENS'
28.6	SOVIET JEWS DENIED EXIT VISAS*
27.8	SALT II TALKS STALLED*
21.7	MISSISSIPPI RIVER REACHES FLOOD STAGE
18.6	U.S. BALANCE OF PAYMENTS GLOOMY*
17.5	STEELERS FAVORED TO WIN SUPER BOWL
12.9	PRESIDENT THREATENS TO VETO APPROPRIATIONS BILL PASSED BY CONGRESS
11.7	SENATE COMMITTEE HEARS TESTIMONY ON CIVIL SER-VICE REGULATIONS
10.3	U.S.-RUSSIAN WOMEN'S BASKETBALL PLAY-OFF EX-PECTED IN OLYMPICS
9.9	REFEREE TURNS McENROE-NASTASE MATCH OVER TO UMPIRE
9.5	NEW LAND SPEED RECORD SET ON SALT FLATS
2.1	PROFESSIONAL SOCCER DRAWING RECORD CROWDS

Another measure of seniors' perceptions of global affairs was a question that asked respondents to rank 10 world problems in order of importance. The median rankings (from most important to least important) by the seniors appear below.

SENIORS' MEDIAN RANKINGS OF IMPORTANCE OF WORLD PROBLEMS

Malnutrition and inadequate health care	3.96
Depletion of natural resources	4.04
Denial of basic human rights	4.05
Nuclear and conventional arms proliferation	4.10
Air and water pollution	5.23
Inflation and unemployment	5.49
Overpopulation	5.65
Terrorism	6.87
Racial discrimination	7.01
Intergroup conflict	8.60

To illustrate the coverage of the knowledge test, 16 questions are reproduced, drawn from each of the topics covered by the test with the exception of Distribution of Natural Characteristics. Representation of the topics is uneven, however, so the questions have been organized into clusters. Questions 1-6 stress the theme of economic development, questions 7-11 aspects of international relations, questions 12-14 ethnicity and religion, and questions 15 and 16 the environment and natural resources.

Below each question, there are statistics that indicate the percentage of the college senior sample that chose each response (or omitted the question) and the performance level of each response group on the total test. (The correct answer is indicated by an asterisk.) The difficulty level of the 16 questions ranges from a low of slightly under 14 percent correct to a high of slightly under 77 percent correct. Overall, the 16 questions are somewhat more difficult than the total test, on which the seniors had a mean score of almost exactly 50 percent correct. The lowest score for the seniors was zero and the highest 84, and about two thirds of the scores fell between 38 and 62. Only 2 percent of the scores were in the "chance" range—that is, scores that could be achieved by marking response options at random.

The first cluster of questions dealt with economic development. For question 2, which had the highest percentage correct of any question among the 16, slightly more than one out of five seniors mistakenly thought that the gap in per capita income between the world's richest and poorest countries had remained the same or narrowed since the Second World War. Question 3 tested whether students understood fundamental population patterns among nations at different stages of development. Slightly less than half the seniors did. Many chose a response option that confused Sweden's postindustrial pattern with the pattern of the United States. Despite this confusion this group did perceive the essential difference between developing nations such as Mexico and industrial or postindustrial nations like the United States or Sweden. Question 4, on the problem of food supply in developing countries, brought to light a major misconception that was echoed on other questions in the test. More than half the seniors, although not the ablest group on the total test, incorrectly thought that these countries have not had the resources to grow enough food to feed their people. Question 5 explored an important impact of the West on revolutionary leaders of the Third World. More than half the seniors correctly perceived that the West's social and political theories have had the most profound influence on those leaders who were educated in the West. Not surprisingly, the next largest group of seniors opted for industrial technology as the biggest influence. The last question in this cluster, number 6, tested for knowledge about issues on which there has been the greatest success in achieving cross-cultural consensus on aims and policies. About half the seniors thought that great success had occurred in areas that are, in fact, highly contentious.

The second cluster, which dealt with international relations, opened with question 7 on the Soviet view of the United States. The seniors did well on this question. Nearly 70 percent chose the correctly stated

A SAMPLING OF NATIONAL TEST QUESTIONS
(asterisk indicates correct answer)

1. The United States accounts for roughly 5 percent of the world's population. The entries on which line (1, 2, 3, or 4) of the table below are approximately correct for the United States today?

	% of World Consumption of Nonrenewable Resources	% of World Production of Economic Goods and Services
(1)	40	25
(2)	10	40
(3)	30	30
(4)	25	5

	OMIT	(1)*	(2)	(3)	(4)	TOTAL
PERCENT	11.65	56.16	7.05	19.76	5.38	100.00
MEAN SCORE	45.34	52.39	42.85	50.60	50.87	50.46

2. Since the Second World War, the gap in per capita income between the world's richest and poorest countries has

    (1) widened
    (2) remained about the same
    (3) narrowed slightly
    (4) narrowed substantially

	OMIT	(1)*	(2)	(3)	(4)	TOTAL
PERCENT	1.15	76.76	6.57	13.06	2.45	100.00
MEAN SCORE	37.40	51.53	49.55	47.70	40.33	50.46

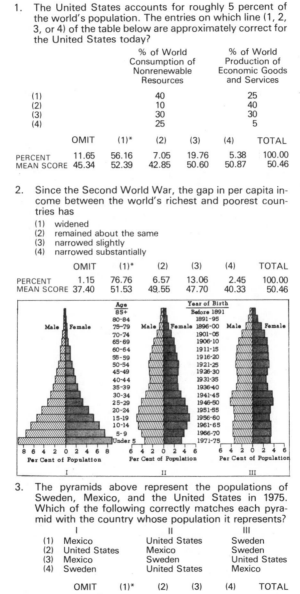

3. The pyramids above represent the populations of Sweden, Mexico, and the United States in 1975. Which of the following correctly matches each pyramid with the country whose population it represents?

	I	II	III
(1)	Mexico	United States	Sweden
(2)	United States	Mexico	Sweden
(3)	Mexico	Sweden	United States
(4)	Sweden	United States	Mexico

	OMIT	(1)*	(2)	(3)	(4)	TOTAL
PERCENT	8.90	48.49	7.98	26.87	7.76	100.00
MEAN SCORE	44.02	53.80	42.02	49.93	47.49	50.46

4. Which of the following is the major reason more and more countries in Asia, Africa, and Latin America have become net food importers in the last 50 years?

(1) Generally they have not had the resources to grow enough food to feed their populations.
(2) They have been encouraged to shift production from food crops to cash crops.
(3) Importing food has seemed desirable as a hedge against frequent crop failures.
(4) They have shifted a large part of the labor force to industrial production.

	OMIT	(1)	(2)*	(3)	(4)	TOTAL
PERCENT	1.73	52.38	19.72	6.15	20.02	100.00
MEAN SCORE	38.25	50.14	56.21	43.93	48.71	50.46

5. Which of the following aspects of Western education has had the most profound influence on revolutionary leaders of the Third World who were educated in the West?

(1) Humanities
(2) Physical and biological sciences
(3) Industrial technology
(4) Social and political theories

	OMIT	(1)	(2)	(3)	(4)*	TOTAL
PERCENT	1.32	3.86	2.12	38.53	54.17	100.00
MEAN SCORE	37.74	49.40	40.92	48.85	52.37	50.46

6. On which of the following issues has there been the greatest success in achieving cross-cultural consensus on aims and policies?

(1) Health, as exemplified by the activities of the World Health Organization (WHO)
(2) Working conditions, as exemplified by the activities of the International Labour Organisation (ILO)
(3) Industrial development, as exemplified by the activities of the United Nations Industrial Development Organization (UNIDO)
(4) Human rights, as exemplified by the activities of the United Nations Economic and Social Council (ECOSOC)

	OMIT	(1)*	(2)	(3)	(4)	TOTAL
PERCENT	3.63	46.21	4.95	29.46	15.75	100.00
MEAN SCORE	37.78	54.61	40.18	49.47	46.31	50.46

7. In its official interpretations of United States foreign policy, Soviet doctrine tends to emphasize which of the following arguments?

(1) The United States is a democracy; consequently, its foreign policy is driven by the aggressive aims of the masses.
(2) The United States is a state under the control of monopoly capitalists, and as such, it is an imperialist power.
(3) The United States is a disguised dictatorship; therefore, its foreign policy reflects the territorial ambitions of its military leaders.
(4) Internal divisions weaken the United States; hence, it is a paper tiger and can safely be defied.

	OMIT	(1)	(2)*	(3)	(4)	TOTAL
PERCENT	3.32	13.42	69.40	5.50	8.36	100.00
MEAN SCORE	29.15	41.50	54.54	42.95	44.33	50.46

official Soviet interpretation of United States foreign policy. Performance fell, however, on number 8, which explored a recent issue in U.S.-Soviet relations. Despite their having expressed in the attitude section of the survey a strong interest in the subject of human rights, less than 30 percent of the seniors could identify the major accomplishment of the Helsinki Accords. Those who answered incorrectly generally assumed far more concrete results from the Helsinki Accords than were in fact achieved. Many mistakenly thought that a court to hear human rights complaints had been established. Questions 9 and 10 were designed to test the student's knowledge of some major developments in the international system during the past three decades—in particular, changes in the patterns of Cold War bloc behavior. Both questions 9 and 10 received an unimpressive correct-response rate of under 30 percent. The final question in this cluster covered the history of international arms control in the twentieth century. Only about a quarter of the seniors knew which of the four factors on lack of progress in this area was least important.

The third cluster, which dealt with ethnicity and religion, contained three questions. Question 12 covered the student's sense of ethnolinguistic diversity in countries around the world. Only 30 percent of the seniors picked India, Nigeria, and Iran as the three states with the greatest diversity. This seems surprising in light of the publicity that has been given the ethnic conflict currently smoldering in Iran. Nearly 50 percent of the seniors thought that Czechoslovakia, Sri Lanka, and the United States was the answer, which may mean that their answers were influenced by the rediscovery and celebration in this country of our ethnic heritage. Question 14 asked students to choose a characteristic that is common to Christianity, Judaism, Islam, Buddhism, and Hinduism. A meager 14 percent were able to do so.

The last cluster concerned environment and natural resources. On question 15, the preponderance of seniors demonstrated a lack of historical perspective on the problem of environmental alteration. They chose urbanization rather than cultivation of crops as the human activity contributing most directly to environmental alteration of the greatest area of the earth's surface during the course of history. Similarly, for question 16, the most popular answer was one that greatly overestimated the duration and extent of the world's past and probable future consumption of fossil fuels. Despite the publicity of the last decade about the nonrenewability of fossil fuels, more than one out of four seniors thought that future consumption of fossil fuels would rise indefinitely.

Although the assessment committee chose questions in what it con-

8. In the area of human rights, the major accomplishment of the Helsinki Accords was the

    (1) establishment of a court where human rights complaints can be heard
    (2) acknowledgment of the signatories' right to intercede in the event one of their members violates human rights
    (3) commitment made by the United States to admit as an immigrant any Eastern European who can show that his or her human rights have been violated
    (4) recognition accorded human rights as a legitimate subject of discussion in the East-West debate

	OMIT	(1)	(2)	(3)	(4)*	TOTAL
PERCENT	17.90	27.41	13.94	12.18	28.57	100.00
MEAN SCORE	43.96	50.95	45.05	45.12	58.97	50.46

9. All of the following are examples of the emergence during the 1960s of a multipolar international system EXCEPT the

    (1) French withdrawal from the NATO command structure
    (2) Sino-Soviet rift
    (3) independent moves in international relations made by Romania
    (4) Cuban Missile Crisis

	OMIT	(1)	(2)	(3)	(4)*	TOTAL
PERCENT	12.07	15.84	10.85	31.83	29.42	100.00
MEAN SCORE	46.07	48.25	46.01	49.83	55.78	50.46

10. Nonalignment in international affairs can best be described as a movement

    (1) fostered by Nehru of India, Nasser of Egypt, and Tito of Yugoslavia, involving the refusal of some countries to be tied to a military alliance with either of the two Cold War blocs
    (2) among some Third World countries to create a third international economic system, neither capitalist nor socialist, aimed at extricating these countries from the economic domination of the United States or the Soviet Union
    (3) fostered by Chou En-lai of China, Castro of Cuba, and Allende of Chile to establish a third significant military bloc capable of restoring a global multipolar balance of power
    (4) among socialist democratic countries to establish their neutrality in the event of war between capitalist democratic powers and totalitarian socialist powers

	(1)*	(2(	(3)	(4)	TOTAL
PERCENT	11.43	29.45	25.83	8.60	24.69	100.00
MEAN SCORE	39.60	57.74	48.98	46.22	49.84	50.46

11. Between 1900 and 1979, numerous conferences and agreements intended to establish the conditions of international peace through prevention and control of war as well as through arms limitation fell short of their aims. Which of the following is LEAST important in explaining the lack of substantial progress toward world peace?

    (1) Sequences of arms buildup, followed by perceived threat, followed by another arms buildup by two rival nations or blocs of nations

(2) Failure to design and implement a system of collective security that nations can trust to preserve their safety and to protect their interests

(3) Destabilizing effects of war-related science and technology on arms limitation agreements

(4) The increase in the number of governments established by military coup and the number of governments currently dominated by military regimes

	OMIT	(1)	(2)	(3)	(4)*	TOTAL
PERCENT	9.18	13.84	26.38	23.63	26.97	100.00
MEAN SCORE	41.78	48.36	49.19	52.51	53.93	50.46

12. Since 1945, political conflict and instability have often arisen as a result of racial, religious, ethnic, and linguistic differences within many states. Of the following, which three states contain within their boundaries the most ethnolinguistic diversity?

(1) Italy, Jamaica, Japan
(2) Czechoslovakia, Sri Lanka, the United States
(3) India, Nigeria, Iran
(4) Panama, Romania, Turkey

	OMIT	(1)	(2)	(3)*	(4)	TOTAL
PERCENT	4.13	11.01	49.23	29.98	5.56	100.00
MEAN SCORE	39.36	44.33	50.11	55.42	47.23	50.46

13. Which of the following is a correct statement about the historical sources of population in North and South America?

(1) During the mid-eighteenth century struggle between England and France for predominance in Canada, the French were a minority of the Canadian white population.

(2) By the beginning of the nineteenth century, all major areas of European settlement on the South American continent were under Spanish domination.

(3) The first sizable number of people of Mexican descent in the United States were resident in areas conquered or annexed by the United States in the mid-nineteenth century.

(4) In the massive influx of European immigrants into the United States during the late nineteenth and early twentieth centuries, Northern Europeans predominated over immigrants from Eastern and Southern Europe.

	OMIT	(1)	(2)	(3)*	(4)	TOTAL
PERCENT	6.44	8.38	19.65	35.13	30.40	100.00
MEAN SCORE	40.79	47.51	48.00	54.32	50.46	50.46

14. Which of the following is shared by Christianity, Judaism, Islam, Buddhism, and Hinduism?

(1) The concept of a messiah
(2) A general tendency to proselytize
(3) A tradition of mysticism
(4) Insistence on personal identification with a single religion

	OMIT	(1)	(2)	(3)*	(4)	TOTAL
PERCENT	3.17	35.11	5.44	13.72	42.56	100.00
MEAN SCORE	39.23	48.14	51.17	53.98	51.98	50.46

15. During the course of history, which of the following human activities has contributed most directly to environmental alteration of the greatest area of the earth's surface?

   (1)   Urbanization
   (2)   Livestock raising
   (3)   Hunting and gathering
   (4)   Cultivation of crops

	OMIT	(1)	(2)	(3)	(4)*	TOTAL
PERCENT	0.48	62.57	3.30	2.20	31.45	100.00
MEAN SCORE	19.10	48.88	46.97	35.63	55.49	50.46

16. Which of the following curves best represents the estimates of experts about the pattern of the world's past and possible future consumption of fossil fuels such as petroleum, natural gas, and coal?

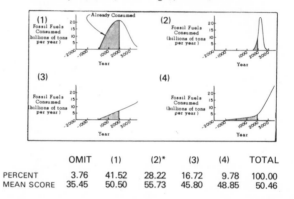

	OMIT	(1)	(2)*	(3)	(4)	TOTAL
PERCENT	3.76	41.52	28.22	16.72	9.78	100.00
MEAN SCORE	35.45	50.50	55.73	45.80	48.85	50.46

sidered an appropriate range of difficulty for each issue, no special effort was made to balance the difficulty of the questions from topic to topic. The relative difficulty of each issue, therefore, reflects the absolute difficulty of the questions as well as the knowledge level of the students.

More illuminating than mean scores on the 13 topics are the correlations between performance on each topic and performance on the total test. The group of topics that stood out as having the closest relationship to the total test included arts and culture (.71), war and armaments (.69), racial and ethnic issues (.67), relations among states (.66), and international monetary and trade arrangements (.65). Religion had the lowest correlation (.37). In between were those topics—distribution of natural characteristics excepted—that have been less traditional, especially in the college curriculum: environment, population, energy, human rights, health, and food.

It is interesting to note that history majors excelled on the test, achieving a mean score of 59.30. Their cousins specializing in the other social sciences scored above the mean (52.77), but they were outdistanced by engineering and mathematics majors (53.2 and 54.07). Particularly disquieting was the last-place finish of education majors, whose mean score was 39.83. Students in vocational/technical training scored 45.00, more than five points above education majors. English/drama/communications majors scored a little less than two points below the mean (48.84), perhaps a reflection of the slant of the test toward the social sciences. Similarly, foreign language majors were just barely below the mean (50.22), quite possibly for the same reason. And finally, business/accounting/finance majors, despite the traditional idea that they have no interest in the liberal arts, scored about a point above the mean (51.35).

A Psychological View of Global Understanding

Item-by-item analyses provide some basic insights into what students know and feel about their world. It seems equally important, however, to fit the pieces together and to determine which survey variables capture the essence of global understanding.

To accomplish this we selected 21 variables that are clearly interpretable and that span the survey's content. Relationships among these variables were then summarized by the complex statistical technique called "factor analysis." Further details appear in the full study report.

Three separate components emerge from this analysis. They are *knowledge, affect,* and *foreign language.* Below each of these three components we have listed those eight survey variables that are most closely associated with the component (see box). Thus the knowledge

---

COMPONENTS OF GLOBAL UNDERSTANDING
(derived from 21 selected variables)

Knowledge	Affect (attitudes, etc.)	Foreign Language
Global Understanding Test Score (89)	Chauvinism Scale (70)	F.L. Speaking Ability (95)
Usually Read International News (43)	World Government Scale (57)	F.L. Listening Ability (91)
International News Headlines (35)	Concern Scale (55)	F.L. Reading Ability (89)
Chauvinism Scale (34)	Cooperation Scale (53)	Extent of Informal Language Learning (61)
Concern Scale (34)	War Scale (50)	Attitude Toward F.L. Learning (59)
Error-Choice Score (30)	Left Political Attitude (44)	Amount of F.L. Study (Grades 7-16) (56)
College Grade Point Average (29)	Human Rights Scale (38)	Concern Scale (42)
Human Rights Scale (28)	Attitude Toward F.L. Learning (36)	Time in Foreign Areas (37)

( )--correlation of variable with factor

---

component is primarily established by the knowledge test score. High correlations include two newspaper information acquisition variables. Minor associations with grade point average, time in foreign areas, and several attitude scales are evident. The knowledge component is defined primarily by the test score and is related to information acquisition via newspaper reading, academic achievement, and attitudes, as we predicted; knowledge is not related to radio and TV news experience.

Foreign language abilities, learning experiences, and attitudes are contained in the language component. As would be expected, one of the student background variables most highly related to language was the amount of formal course work taken in the junior high school, high school, and college years. Also strongly associated with language were contact activities outside the formal U.S. educational context, including speaking a foreign language with family members, friends, or neighbors. Foreign language proficiency was also moderately associated with student responses to the attitude scale for "concern."

Quite surprising on first observation was the absence of any substantial relationship between language proficiency and level of knowledge of world issues. One possible explanation of this finding could be that, of the number of students in the total sample, the great majority had not reached a level of proficiency in the foreign language sufficient to permit any meaningful use of relevant information sources in the foreign language (for example, conversations with native speakers, foreign radio or TV broadcasts, newspapers, news magazines, and other publications in the foreign language) that could have led to a higher and more sophisticated acquaintance with important world issues. Additional analyses are planned to determine whether there is a "threshold" level of language proficiency beyond which appreciable relationships with global knowledge are observed.

The final component for interpretation, affect, was established by a cluster of variables that is totally unsurprising from a conceptual point of view and from pretest work. More interesting was the relationship between "left" political attitudes and the more specific attitudes that were included as direct components of the global understanding domain. A "left" political orientation would appear to be associated with the concerned, cooperative, pro-world-government, pro-human-rights, antiwar, and antichauvinistic sentiments tapped by our scales. Note that error-choice did not have an appreciable relationship with the affect component. At this point, we would have to say that the technique did not work as expected. Further analyses are planned.

Turning to relationships among the three factors, we should underscore the clear distinction and lack of overlap between knowledge and language. Note that language variables did not relate to the knowledge component and that the knowledge score did not relate to the language component. Affect, on the other hand, seemed to overlap moderately with knowledge and, to a lesser extent, with language, as indicated by those variables common to knowledge and affect and to language and affect, respectively.

Correlations among the three factors were moderate to low, which indicated that the domains corresponding to the factors were fairly distinct. The relative sizes of the correlations suggest the oversimplified diagram below.

This diagram extends our powers of interpretation to the limit but provides a satisfying picture. One must remember, however, that the low-level association between language and knowledge was due to links through affect and that the relationship between the knowledge test score and self-assessed language ability was essentially zero. These findings are considerably elaborated in the final report.

Chapter 5

Forward to Basics: Education as Wide as the World

Harlan Cleveland

"**B**ack to Basics." This persuasive slogan hangs in heavy political air and influences every discussion of the future of American education. But to define the necessary basics for today's young people, we also need to look forward, to guess at the future in which they will have to function.

We have not yet found a generally accepted name to characterize the period we are in transition *to*—for my taste, "postindustrial" is too retrospective a tag for so different and exciting a future, and too economic a name for a period in which the analysis of political, cultural, and psychological dynamics will also be vital to an understanding of the world.

The transition comprises a wide variety of changes in beliefs, loyalties, fears, aspirations, and doctrines, and some very fundamental shifts in assumptions about the definition of resources, the purposes of growth, the nature of security, and the concept of equity (or fairness). We are proceeding, it seems,

- *From* an ethic of quantitative growth (measured and symbolized by that grotesque index, the GNP) *to* an ethic of quality and stability and control of one's own destiny.
- *From* the inner logic of technological progress and the invisible hand of the market *to* social direction setting for new technologies and political bargaining as the force in the marketplace.
- *From* preoccupation with physical limits to growth *to* a new emphasis on recycling of nonrenewable resources, on biological resources (because they're renewable), and on information as an expandable resource.
- *From* planning as scientific management or management engineering (which brought us PPBS as the *reductio ad absurdum*) *to* concepts of planning as pluralistic improvisation on a general sense of direction.
- *From* colonial rule and industrial leadership *to* a global fairness revolution.

- *From* a balance of power based on certainty *to* a balance of power that depends for its stability on mutual uncertainty.
- *From* concepts of security as military defense *to* concepts of security as including oil, environmental risks, nuclear proliferation, population growth, inflation, unsafe streets, and Islamic revolutions.
- *From* local and national technologies *to* inherently global technologies (for weather observation, military reconnaissance, telecommunications, data processing, remote sensing, orbital industries, etc.) and as a result:
- *From* concepts of national ownership, sovereignty, and citizenship *to* ideas like the ocean commons, international monitoring of environmental risks, and the common heritage of man.

That is only a start. Each of us can—indeed, we had all better —make our own lists. But whatever our particular perspectives, we find a common characteristic: Our concepts are all widening out to include what used to be regarded as externalities—a fancy word for factors that simply fit no traditional discipline or profession or analytical system yet seem to be disturbingly relevant.

We are coming to realize that whenever we make avoidable trouble for ourselves, Abe Lincoln and Walt Kelly in their different formulations were right in fingering the enemy as us. We find it seductively comforting to tunnel our vision, to focus too sharply on one issue at a time and neglect to ask questions that illuminate the ways in which, as the study of ecology has now taught us, everything is related to everything else. We plunged into the use of nuclear power for electricity without asking the hard questions about the back end of the nuclear fuel cycle—about safety, about waste, about proliferation. We pursued growth without asking, "Growth for what?" and, "Growth for whom?" We were persuaded by narrow-gauge, straight-line extrapolations that we were running out of resources, when we were running out of imagination.

We applauded a goal of national energy independence when the problem was the management of international energy interdependence. We produced new gadgets and only then inquired about their consequences. We built highways and discovered only later their effect on urban living. We built on land without asking how the nearby weather would be thereby modified. Some corporations neglected their social responsibilities, induced consumer outrage expressed in government regulation, and then wondered how that army of regulators happened to become so intrusive and so burdensome.

In international affairs the effect of tunneling our vision, working hard on the detailed tactics and not on a strategy that relates the disparate parts of our foreign policy to each other, is even more calamitous. We have recently been given many object lessons, from our invasion of Cambodia in spring 1970, through the collision of human rights with arms control, to the hostage politics of the eighties.

We suffer just now from a vacuum of general strategy—a larger and more damaging vacuum in a generation mostly spent observing and practicing diplomacy. Historians may say of the seventies that in the first part of the decade there were leaders in Washington who did bad things on purpose, while in the latter part of the decade there were leaders in Washington who did good things and did not relate them to each other—and that worked out almost as badly.

I confidently predict that in order to cope with the worldwide complexities of American citizenship, all of us, in and out of education, will have to widen our perspectives well beyond our particular disciplines, professions, departments, and even our nationalities. Whatever one's line of work, it will be more needful in the future to be interdisciplinary, interprofessional, interdepartmental, and international. Otherwise we will be out of touch with the realities in which we live and survive.

Most of us are very badly prepared to live and work in an environment where there will evidently be a high premium on long-range vision, strategic thinking, and the wider view. Yet educators of the eighties and nineties are responsible for making sure that Americans enter the twenty-first century with a view as wide as the world. The implication is far reaching: The widest and most neglected frontier of U.S. educational reform is no longer international studies. It is a global perspective on *all* studies.

The notion that the whole curriculum of formal education, at each level from the preschool to postdoctoral, should be taught and learned in international perspective is not at all a substitute for—and should not be a threat to—international studies and foreign language training. These are and will remain valid and increasingly important specialties. But competent American citizenship in an interdependent world cannot come from stuffing into the schools' curricula another course or two about foreign areas and faraway cultures. It will come from a generation of students relearning in each course they take, on every subject, at every level of education, that the world is round (and fully packed, too)—that everything Americans do or do not do affects the rest of the world, and everything others do bears watching for its effect on our own lives, our own purposes, and our own destiny.

There is a teacher on Cape Cod who found she could introduce third graders to arithmetic fractions by using as problems the swings in international currency exchange rates—simplified, of course, to remove the decimal points and other adult refinements. Smuggling a beginning course in the international monetary system into a roomful of nine-year-olds: That is creative education. But why smuggle it in? Why not decriminalize such ventures in educational creativity?

Nor should a global perspective in education be viewed as a rival to, or substitution for, the basics. Schoolchildren should learn to read, write, count, and cooperate—and so should college students and graduate students if, as too often happens, they missed these skills earlier on. But the basics can be learned in ways that encourage narrower or wider understanding of the world about us. It is basic that students should learn to read and write what is relevant, to count what counts, and not grow up thinking that what cannot be counted does not count. Students need to learn not only the techniques but the purposes of cooperation. Reading, writing, and arithmetic, science, humanities, and social studies are all basics, but the content of the basics has to shift with the times. What is basic in our time is the need for international competence. Not "Back to Basics" but "Forward to Basics" should be printed on the placards of the next generation's reformers.

My impression is that we are farther along in widening our perspectives in kindergarten and elementary and even in the high schools than we are in higher education. In the early grades, after all, the students have not yet been persuaded that the world is made up of the sum of categorical expertnesses. Dividing knowledge into specialties and walling them off from each other is not the natural condition of the integrative human mind. Like racial prejudice, walling off knowledge has to be carefully taught.

For the K-12 level of schooling a good deal of creative work has been done these past few years to demonstrate how existing courses can be converted to reflect the new requirement for global perspectives. The stimulation of new conceptual thinking has led to practical field tests and teacher training exercises in New York, San Francisco, Indiana, Minnesota, Colorado, New Mexico, and elsewhere. These efforts have begun to flesh out the skeleton of an idea.

But the academic revolution inherent in global perspectives in education is pervasive, and is equally crucial for the colleges and universities. High schoolers who have learned to think in these wider ways may be wondering out loud, when they get to college, why the higher education establishment has not yet internalized the interconnections between its parochial concerns and the wide, turbulent, and exciting world which will so deeply affect the students' personal destinies for good or ill.

Some of us were hoping for more recognition of this comparatively fresh theme in the report of the President's Commission on Foreign Language and International Studies. Its absence is some indication of how far U.S. education still has to go in rethinking its mission in the age of global satellites, global hunger, global weapons, and global ayatollahs. Nonetheless, I agree with just about everything the commission did recommend in its effort to generate more support for the more traditional language and area studies and for instruction about international relations. It simply did not go far enough.

It is true that I have long been skeptical of the too easy assumption that linguistic skill, cultural empathy, and political acumen are likely to be found in the same package. Twenty years ago, in a Maxwell School study for the Carnegie Corporation, we reported having found a disturbingly large number of "fluently arrogant" Americans abroad. Our reference to arrogant fluency caused quite a stir in the Modern Language Association at the time; one whole session of MLA was devoted to criticisms of our 1960 book on *The Overseas Americans*. (The authors were grateful, of course, since it helped the sales of the book.)

A positive correlation between fluency and arrogance is still to be found in the international exchange of persons, and not only among Americans. But while language learning is not a sufficient condition for cross-cultural understanding, it is a necessary condition of global perspective. It is especially useful if the language learning is embedded in a total experience, including the learner's immersion in a situation where everybody else already speaks the language the student is trying to learn.

I also do not want to be caught opposing area studies. But only too often they fail to attract the very best scholars in the relevant disciplines. At times they have, and especially in the Middle East, become partisans in regional conflicts—sometimes lured by grants and contracts that substitute polemics for analysis. Above all, they have tended to emphasize how different each world region is from every other world region, and thereby failed to teach Americans and the U.S. government how strategically similar throughout the developing world—if tactically different in each culture and society—has been the triple collision of technology-driven modernization, rising demands for equity or fairness, and rising resentment of cultural patriots and religious traditionalists.

Indeed, we can now see how misleading this tendency to divide the world among geographic regions can be that so deeply affected the organization not only of university programs but of the foreign affairs agencies of the federal government. We—the American people and their government alike—got firmly in our heads that geographic contiguity was the main organizing principle for understanding, and therefore dealing with, the non-American world. In consequence we have neglected the *functional regionalism* that is so much more interesting, relevant, and dangerous in the management of world order politics.

OPEC and OECD are now much more important to our destiny than the geographically regional institutions of, say, Africa or the Western Hemisphere. Brazil and Mexico, for example, seem much more interested in their relations with other industrial countries wherever situated, and are giving the back of their hand to hemispheric cooperation, whether in the Organization of American States or of the Latin-American-only variety. Similarly, the membership in OPEC of Venezuela and Nigeria seems a more important part of their foreign policy than their Latin American and African nonsolidarity.

The declining relevance of geographical proximity, in this age of jet travel, satellite telecommunication, and supersonic weapons, is only one of several intellectual rigidities that are getting in our way as we try to train ourselves for international competence.

Our attempt to export American distinctions between public and private enterprises, and thus between government and business, is proving to be equally unhelpful as we watch government-business cooperation in Japan and Germany outstripping our rates of growth and productivity. This is familiar terrain. But two other anachronisms, not yet so widely recognized, also get in our way: the notion that most international relations are bilateral, and our dysfunctional distinction between international affairs and domestic affairs.

We are still organized (not just in our society but in our own minds) to deal with other nations bilaterally when nearly all international decision making has now become multilateral. I recently asked Saburo Okita, the international economist appointed in 1980 as Japan's foreign minister, whether the world looked different from his seat of authority. He was impressed, he said, by the obsolescence of one-on-one relations between countries. Nearly every issue now involves several countries; decisions are made in multilateral negotiations at many-sided tables.

When I was ambassador to NATO, I frequently visited my bilateral colleagues in Europe, and observed that 60 to 75 percent of the substantive issues on the bilateral ambassador's desk were being decided, not in a *pas de deux* between the United States and one diplomatic partner, but in a wider circle of the concerned. That is, in the U.N., in the Atlantic Alliance, in GATT or EEC or others of the half a hundred intergovernmental organizations to which the United States then belonged, through some of the 700 intergovernmental conferences to which the United States sent official representatives each year. A study by the British Foreign Office confirms this impression. In a bilateral embassy, the British say, 75 percent of the business is essentially multilateral.

This multilateralization of world affairs should—but does not—deeply affect the way we teach and learn in school and college, and the way we operate in international business and in the nonprofit "third system." By their nature, as most now realize, multinational corporations operate in more and more multilateral ways. The effect of multilateralism in the nonprofit sector has received rather less attention.

The exchange-of-persons programs were mostly born in the earlier era of primarily bilateral relations. Some of them are still stuck in that groove, but others are increasingly trying to reflect in their workways the new environment, which is that policy issues mostly require personal relationships among several or many different cultures and nationalities, not merely two. The Eisenhower Fellowships and the Humphrey Fellowships both bring together in the United States midcareer people from many countries in a common program. So does the East-West Center in Hawaii, which stirs different kinds of Asians with Americans in combined research efforts. The American Field Service, the Experiment in International Living, and Youth for Understanding have, in recent years, been trying to make sure that, even in their essentially bilateral exchanges, the students get some exposure to the multilateralization of problems and solutions. The YMCA has been trying to introduce international perspectives into the programs of its local constituents, not as an add-on specialty but as part of each Y's basic program.

And where have the schools, colleges, and universities been all this time? A comparative study might show that, of all American institutions, they are still the most resistant to this trend.

The most important and damaging distinction that gets in our way, as we redefine competence for American citizens in an interdependent world, is that thick black line we have drawn in our minds and in our institutions between international affairs and domestic affairs. Among traditional diplomats in formal meetings there may still be a pretense that world politics and the world economy consist of the relations between monoliths called nations. But educators do not need to be so uncandid. In practice, the content of international affairs is now mostly the domestic affairs of still sovereign countries.

Taking a single example, North-South relations—that grab bag of many subjects which bears on the gaps and conflicts between the world's richer and poorer peoples—the point is simply made. The developing countries want some hard decisions made inside the economies of the industrial democracies. (The Soviet Union, Eastern Europe, and China are still sitting out this particular dance.) The desired decisions have to do with insuring access to our big markets; making sure North America grows and stores enough grain for the world food system; and getting the industrial countries to work hard on usable development technologies, to transfer resources as development assistance, to manage their powerful economies so as not to export inflation, and to regulate the international operations of multinational companies.

Each of these areas for decision is sensitive, politically charged, and traditionally regarded as the province of domestic politics. The main forces engaged are not bureaucracies and legislatures, but labor unions wanting to protect domestic jobs, business communities wanting to protect profit margins, farm lobbies wanting to protect high prices, environmental movements wanting to protect nature, and consumer groups wanting to protect their purchasing power. These and other special-interest groups have the demonstrated capacity to bring government to a halt—and even to bring governments down. The internal politics of the industrial nations need to be faced frankly and discussed out loud.

At the same time, people in the industrial North are going to need assurance that their efforts to help are effective in doing something about poverty in the South. Poverty is first of all a matter of domestic institutions that discriminate, structurally and systematically, against the poor. Doing something about poverty requires first of all hard decisions *inside* the political economies of developing countries—decisions about land tenure, rural reconstruction, basic-needs strategy, education, productivity incentives, and the widening of participation in decision making. Since those in charge in poor countries are not usually poor themselves, they also have something to protect, and that often does not lead to a vigorous war on poverty.

The basis for planetary bargaining, or whatever we choose to call the pluralistic processes of world order, is arrangements that provide assurances to each participating nation about the kinds of *internal* reform and restructuring in other nations that can make positive-sum *in-*

ternational relations possible. American citizens, who are bound to be active participants in local decisions with global consequences, should not be crippled by learning in school and college to segregate domestic and foreign policies in separate compartments.

One of the first things the first secretary of education did was to appoint a task force to address the question of international competence. It was the right move, at past the right time. Each morning's newspaper and each evening's newscast reinforces the need for citizen competence. We must find ways to equip American citizens with the knowledge, skills, and attitudes they will need to function effectively as human beings and policy makers in an increasingly interdependent world.

The requirement is clear enough. What seems to be strangely unclear is that this citizen competence is not only, or even mostly, a matter of learning *about* international affairs. It is learning to relate what goes on abroad to one's own life and work—and, just as important, vice versa.

As Stephen K. Bailey has put it, a humanistic education is one that reaches out for friends in the vast threatening environment that surrounds us. We seem to be rather short of dependable friends just now. Maybe part of the reason is that we are not educating ourselves to reach out for them.

Chapter 6

Expanding International Dimensions

Wesley W. Posvar

L iving in the late twentieth century is a hazardous adventure. Ours is not the only generation ever to have sensed that we live on the edge of doom, but we surely have more hard evidence than ever before to prove it. I regard this as the underlying reason for this discourse on the Council on Learning's Education and the World View program.

The stakes are so high around the world that one feels compelled to begin by reciting a litany of risks. We are increasingly preoccupied with accelerating trends toward asymptotes of catastrophe: an exploding population, dwindling energy, endemic hunger, expanding terror, and the statistical probability of a nuclear holocaust—unless there is some systemic change in the way national governments behave toward one another.

There are also aspects of hope and opportunity in the world view: Our planet has gone through a remarkable process of shrinkage; the time for circumnavigation of the globe has been reduced 1,000 times —or four orders of magnitude—in the past two centuries. Hence this discussion carries an urgent purpose and must aspire to sensible outcomes.

A marvelous moment in history was the Apollo mission of 1968, when man had his first glimpse of his entire planet. As Archibald MacLeish put it, "To see the earth as we now see it, small and blue and beautiful in that eternal silence where it floats, is to see ourselves as riders on the earth together, brothers on that bright loveliness in the unending night—brothers who *see* now they are truly brothers."

The horizons of the intellect were permanently changed by that magnificent view from outer space; in turn a new dimension was added to the mission of higher education. For all the practical difficulties involved in expanding and strengthening international education, we must now bear firmly in mind the fact that the world view is now and for all time an intrinsic perception.

For the academic community this world crisis must also be seen against the background of the dismal decline of funding support for international studies and programs. The fight for financial survival is now widespread. The National Defense Education Act is in perennial jeopardy; Peace Corps volunteers and Fulbright Scholars are down; foundations and the Agency for International Development have backed away from educational objectives; and of total philanthropy by U.S. corporations and foundations, only 2 percent goes to international programs. The President's Commission on Foreign Language and International Studies has made a ringing and appropriate call for linking international education to national and international security, and for making the national commitments and educational investments that are urgently required.

At my own university—and I believe this is true of higher education in general—dealing with the international dimension transcends matters of curriculum, and even of budget, organizational structure, and faculty politics. There exists deep enthusiasm for this undertaking, and our concerns on the campus lie at the very center of the grand issues involved.

The topic is important at many levels. As Harlan Cleveland discusses elsewhere in this volume, the international system itself is in a state of change. Higher education is not only a part of that change, but could also be an active factor in shaping its outcome. We are not simply tooling up for new tasks. There is an implicit responsibility for higher education to deal effectively with the world view, and along with it a marvelous opportunity, the chance to stretch and mold universities and colleges into a new kind of public service.

Our responsibility is affected by the fact that the international system is being profoundly altered by new elements of communications and relations, "transnational" and often nongovernmental in character. Instant global communications and rapid air travel link peoples in a host of ways, involving multinational corporations, publications, foundations, and multiple associations, which in some ways importantly affect even such abstract factors as ideology, theology, and revived senses of ethnicity.

American colleges and universities themselves constitute a key part of the new transnationalism. What come to mind are the widespread international exchanges of students, professors, and research experts. Our foreign student population in the United States now exceeds a quarter of a million. American students and faculty now swarm across the continents in uncounted numbers. American higher education has become an agent for massive export of knowledge—all kinds of talent, skills, and leadership, delivered abroad and to foreign students at home. We enjoy a very favorable balance of payments in terms of our educational commodities.

Transnational intellectual networks have significant potential for the prevention or reduction of international conflict. In the interest of U.S.-Iranian relations, the personal connections between academics of both countries can be a favorable factor. Those knowledgeable about the Middle East agree that once the intelligentsia of Israel and Egypt form collegial links, they will prove most difficult to sunder. At world congresses of educators, persons assigned by their governments to climb on stage and parrot dogmatic defenses of violations of freedom are punished by the tacit sanctions of their peers.

There is another pattern of involvement by American higher education in world affairs: the many ways in which academics individually serve their government. It is noteworthy that many of the temporary occupants of high posts connected with foreign affairs, including most of our Presidential national security assistants, had served as professors of international relations. This fact alone may not cause much public joy, but it does credit the idea of expertise in foreign affairs.

Given the postwar changes in the international arena, a comprehensive university cannot exist as such, and cannot even respectably be so called, without a powerful set of international studies, international programs, and international relationships, direct and indirect—the international dimension. There are some great universities without law schools or medical schools, or even football teams. But there are no great universities without a strong international dimension. Similarly, colleges and community colleges must expand their own horizons, commensurate with their capabilities.

This dimension was not conceivable for the universities of the Middle Ages, or even for those of the past several centuries. Although universities of the past attempted to deal with universal issues of the intellect, their known world was limited, and late twentieth-century capacities for international communication and for global crisis were largely unimagined.

The expanded mission is not so complex as it is pervasive. It must encompass relationships between undergraduate and graduate education, between area studies and general studies, between theory and application, between teaching and research, and between international courses and greater international scope in many kinds of courses. The need is not to pile on new academic programs but to appreciate and extend the new academic dimension.

Today "hard" disciplines such as physics, chemistry, and mathematics interact and function on an international scale; not to be in touch with the world is possibly for them to miss the leading elements of change. In the disciplines of the social sciences, relationships within or among economics, politics, sociology, history, and anthropology are now meaningless unless made relevant to and understood in a transnational or international framework. In the humanities we remain concerned with and interested in the fundamentals, the sources, the roots of any given culture, but we are inexorably brought to deal as well with the cultural foundations of political and economic institutions.

One cannot begin to understand the politics of India without some sense of Hindu religion and philosophy—nor the powerful economics of Japan without deep attention to its historic sociological origins. The Marxism of Russia and the Marxism of China bear the imprints of the tsars and the emperors, of Marx himself, and of each political state upon the other. The ferment of old religion is now capable of explosive force in the area of mass and instant communication. In the case of Islam we are witnessing today a classically conservative religion and proud culture erupting into what may become a radically new transnational mode or variety of modes. Textbook authors are going to have to rush into heavy rewrites, with scant notion of what to say.

International studies are more than a collection of various regional programs and centers, and even more than the sum of all parts. Along with area studies, each having its appropriate aspects of politics, sociology, history, language, and culture of regions or countries, it is also essential to study global phenomena from the standpoints of disciplines, as in international economics, international politics, international sociology, international communications, and history in an international framework. These should be supplemented by the issues studies, mentioned in the report of the President's commission, such as "energy" and "hunger" and "peace studies."

Beyond these it is important that an international component be added to many courses that have not been traditional parts of international studies programs. General faculty interests and competence should be internationalized. This will be difficult, but there are ways to try.

Language study is the hallmark of international programs and is crucial to the world view in higher education. We all deplore the decline in foreign language capacity among American college and university students. The President's commission called for broadened language study for the cultural enrichment of Americans themselves. "... For many, such knowledge is in its own right a deeply rewarding and fulfilling experience. For all, it will become increasingly important."

The President's commission goes on to say that "...nothing less is at issue than the nation's security.... The United States requires far more reliable capacities to communicate with its allies, analyze the behavior of potential adversaries, and earn the trust and the sympathies of the uncommitted. Yet there is a widening gap between these needs and the American competence to understand and deal successfully with other peoples in a world in flux." The deficiency is serious in West and East Europe. It is particularly grievous in Asia, where virtually all American conversation with foreigners is of necessity with bilingual persons on the other side. The deficiency is disastrous in regions where American interests are being closed out, such as the Horn of Africa and South Asia. A tiny number of Americans fluent in Farsi, Pashto, or Baluchi, for example, could have been or could yet be of incalculable strategic value.

To the voluminous debate on this subject I add the simple observation that we could benefit from a two-tiered system of language training. We should not try to emulate the multilingual academic preparation of Europeans. The mass of Americans, even college students, simply do not have the inclination or the need to be fluently multilingual for their pleasure or business travel. It would be nice if 15 or 20 million more Americans became proficient in at least one other language. But I believe it is far more important that several hundred thousand more Americans become familiar with selected foreign languages and cultures so that they can properly represent our country abroad in business, journalism, diplomacy, politics, the military, and, of course, scholarship. It is crucial that some Americans be experts in understanding the more remote cultural sectors of the planet. If this had been the case in the past, some of the tragic American political misjudgments and failed military interventions might have been either avoided or remedied.

As for the main body of American college students, we might well develop new courses of study for what one might call cultural appreciation—the kind of insight and respect and intellectual humility that emerge as a result of discovery and awareness of cultural differences, especially reinforced by knowledge of the values and manner of thinking and communication of a foreign culture. This would not lead to speaking French with a good accent, to give an example, but it would call for understanding the structure of the French language and its logical precepts, as well as French culture.

Another important aspect is the science of linguistics, and theory and research related to the process of learning language. Pedagogy in the teaching of foreign languages has significance, and it has been a frequent battleground among academicians. Part of the problem has been less than effective teaching, coupled with student frustration over the "irrelevance" of what is taught. Part of the solution may be the newer methods of language acquisition in an environment of ease, confidence, and, yes, fun.

At my own institution some experts feel that we may be approaching the threshold of a science of learning, and we have interested persons in the departments of psychology, philosophy, psychiatry, mathematics, linguistics, and our Learning Research and Development Center. Improving understanding of the capacity for and the process of language acquisition is a very important component of exploration on the frontier of the human mind.

How is significant change to be brought about? The first element of any strategy for expanding the international dimension must be interest and commitment at key levels of administration, in addition to vigorous and devoted academic leaders who can carry out academic programs. National encouragement in this regard comes from the very publication of this volume and from growing discussion about international education among academic presidents, vice presidents, and deans at meetings of major educational associations.

The academic department remains the central link between the university and the disciplines, and also sometimes the stronghold of orthodoxy. A basic challenge therefore is to integrate the relationships between academic disciplines organized into departments, and international studies as a broad range of activities involving people in various departments, and even some people not in departments but in interdisciplinary research units.

In most cases institutions find that they need a "matrix" scheme of organization and administration, wherein the faculties of departments and of whole schools are organized in vertical depth so they can achieve desirable specialization. Other kinds of academic activities that involve members of disciplines in coordinated and cooperative ways are spread horizontally across a span of departments.

In any large academic organization there is also need for some wide-ranging coordinating and facilitating mechanism for international studies. This mechanism should not have a narrow focus; it should affect all interested parts of the institution. At Pittsburgh we call ours the University Center for International Studies. It functions like a holding company, housing regional and functional study programs and promoting exchanges. It also encourages expansion of the international content of all possible conventional courses and curricula, universitywide.

Given sufficient interest and budget by faculty and administration, a few elements may be sought for extending international dimensions:

- The coordinating mechanism described earlier.
- A core curriculum requirement for international relations or foreign language courses, or some innovative combination thereof.
- Involvement of senior and graduate faculty and area
studies specialists in teaching undergraduate students.
There is no simple formula for bringing this about, but one
way may be through an honors program which we have
found makes it exciting for senior faculty and specialists to
teach undergraduates.
- Enrollment of qualified foreign students who would become involved in the broader social and academic life of
the campus. Professional counseling and support services
for them are essential.
- Encouragement of academically creditable study abroad,
usually available for even the smallest colleges via consor-
tia or joint programs.
- Articulation agreements between larger universities and
smaller four-year and two-year colleges, to make more
widely available people competent in international studies.
The American Universities Field Staff provides remarkable
overseas expertise to its small number of member institutions; variations of this scheme could be emulated among
groups of institutions within regions.
- Persuasion of counseling and placement offices of the
importance of foreign language and international studies.
They should also be encouraged to preach the enlightened
v ɔrd to corporate clients. (This is largely uncharted terri-
tory.)

At the heart of all considerations of international curricula must be
the concern with theory: identification and examination of components of the international system and of the streams of communication
that influence the flow of information and ideas among them; formu-
lation of concepts intended to develop a better understanding of how
the international system functions and the directions in which it may
be headed; questioning the meaning of "system" itself, and whether or
how that term applies.
In this sense American higher education has long excelled. Despite
all of the negative or declining development in international and foreign language studies, critics must appreciate that, in the conceptual
study of international relations and in the development of theory,

American scholars became dominant following World War II and remain relatively in the lead.

One group of such scholars developed into "stategic thinkers," who helped form sophisticated views of international security through arms control and policies of strategic deterrence, even as they are variously at work today examining the pitfalls and profound dangers that can lie in such policies. Despite failings among them, the net positive contribution of academic strategy expertise is of welcome importance. In the campaign for advancing the cause of international education, the great professors and theoreticians of international relations should themselves be mobilized, should speak out, and should lead.

Education and the World View opens a new phase of higher education. It is a challenge without parallel—with the added factor that successful improvement of the international order is imperative. The alternative is simply unthinkable. Educators involved in this effort are entitled not only to full funding and support from others. They are also likely to benefit from the highest sense of mission. The goal is nothing less than a functioning though crowded planet, making a secure passage through space and time.

Chapter 7

The New Curricular Equation

Frederick Rudolph

Some years back, a colleague in the history department at Williams and I were given permission to teach a course with the modest title, The Negro in American History. The title itself suggests that the course was not exactly inspired by any widespread interest or pressure: The only black student who took it that first year was a young African who had come to Williams to play soccer. As for us, the reason two of us asked to teach the course jointly was that, while my junior colleague possessed the expertise, I possessed the tenure and therefore presumably the power of persuasion.

Our purpose was not to launch an Afro-American studies program (although there now is one), but instead to find out for ourselves what would happen to American history if blacks were seen as something more than simply a cause of the Civil War. We were not interested in segregating Negro history from American history. We were interested in testing the generalizations that had informed our teaching of American history against the experiences of black Americans. We wanted to find out what we needed to do to reshape and restructure our teaching of American history so as to make it less narrow and parochial. Eventually that course developed another purpose, but by the time it was required to support the consciousness and identity of an increasing number of black students, it had fulfilled its original intention and had served as a laboratory for rethinking all of the college's offerings in American history.

This experience may be instructive for anyone who is concerned about the role of the undergraduate curriculum in shaping students' views of the world. If nothing else, it is encouraging as an inexpensive model, now that major new curricular efforts must confront shrinking institutional budgets. It should not be necessary to throw great sums of money around to make American college students aware of the world. President Carter's call for draft registration may in fact already have done that. What is needed is some sensitive attention to the ways in which a college or university intentionally or accidentally acknowledges the world as a dimension of its particular learning experience.

Chancellor Posvar's challenging chapter, with its appropriate emphasis on how best to organize the university in the interest of global awareness, allows me to focus on ways in which existing and potential capabilities for international studies can be translated into reality. It is our purpose, I believe, to assure this country a supply of leaders with an awareness of the declining relative importance of the United States in world affairs and a sensitivity to the rising importance of nations and peoples once thought of only as subjects for consideration by the *National Geographic* Magazine. We need both an informed populace and a trained leadership; we need a nation of human beings who can recognize in the currrent economic agonies of Detroit a lesson in international economics and global politics, as well as experts and leaders who will not allow us to miss the point of the lesson that Detroit is unhappily teaching us.

The question that Dr. Posvar raises as to whether an institution of higher learning can be great without a powerful international dimension is one that I prefer to avoid. International centers and programs may indeed help to define a university and surely constitute a source of national understanding and wisdom on matters of international significance, but the existence of such centers does not guarantee a strong global dimension in the American undergraduate course of study. On the other hand, what does, what can?

My guess is that we can learn a good deal about what to do and how to do it from the national experience with area studies and modern languages. Both are in trouble, but not for the same reason. The area programs of the 1960s in Russian, African, Chinese, and Latin-American studies were a product of foundation enthusiasm, government grants, and a certain nervousness about the future of American foreign policy and our general success in war and commerce. Because they were almost wholly synthetic and required almost everywhere the bringing together of a cluster of specialists who had not yet mastered the principle or the appropriateness of some integrating concept, these programs—in the absence of widespread student demand—collapsed when financial support began to wither. Modern languages are in trouble not only because schools and colleges no longer subsidize them with requirements, but also because of the generally hostile attitude of literature professors to the teaching and learning of languages.

There is more to the difficulties that beset area studies and foreign languages, of course, than I have here suggested, but the lessons for those who would nudge the undergraduate course of study toward a more responsible role in challenging American ethnocentrism are clear. The world view, global awareness, the international dimension, must grow out of a perceived need and a widely shared purpose: The curriculum must be subjected to the same kind of examination that has brought belated recognition to blacks and women as legitimate and essential areas of study. Once that is done, once we confront the opportunity, there will no doubt be some remarkable discoveries about ways in which the traditional curriculum can embrace a shrinking and changing world and incorporate it into the undergraduate experience.

Dr. Posvar is absolutely right in recognizing the academic department as the crucial source of either innovation or inertia. At my own college the departments of history and religion require some non-Western courses in their major programs, while the art department, although offering courses in Chinese and Indian art, will permit its majors to study entirely in the Western tradition. Yet it is a mistake to think that departments cannot be circumvented or successfully challenged. College and university policies that encourage study abroad are certainly one marvelous source of global awareness. We have a long tradition and expectation in the American civilization program at Williams that our seniors will take a consecutive pair of major seminars. While writing this, I was confronted by two students who for good academic reasons wanted to spend the first term of their senior year in Europe. I balked, reacting as tradition required me to, and then reminded myself of what I was working on: The students went to Europe.

My suspicion is that in other ways students are going to sense the broader changes that are upon us and push in directions toward which they and we ought to go. Some of this push will be unconscious and accidental. Recently I heard the president of Columbia Pictures, at a student showing of a current feature, explain how his liberal arts education, his major in history, and his foreign language study had helped him in his career. Surely some students previously hostile to language study must have recognized the significance of his message that 40 percent of the audience for American-made films is overseas, or of the news that jobs in American companies are going begging because of a lack of young men and women who are proficient in another language.

I thought I was being particularly responsible to the mission of the Council on Learning when I included in the syllabus of my senior American studies seminar on Contemporary America Ezra Vogel's challenging and important book, *Japan as No. 1*. I had already begun the course with Hedrick Smith's *The Russians*, but how far can one go? Yet what really made Vogel's book a happy addition to the course was the imagination of one young woman in the class who brought along a friend, a special student from Japan spending the year at Williams as a protege of the Japanese foreign office. *Japan as No. 1?* There was not a student in that class who was not instantly conscious of how poorly he or she would have done if positions had been reversed with that articulate, gentle, and admirably informed young man from Japan. It may have been too late for those second-term seniors to pick up Japanese as a second language, but I would not be surprised if, at this reading, more than one of them is responding to Berlitz advertisements.

I am wary of the massive dollar solution to our problem, even if that were now possible. My preference is for the more difficult and more lasting solution that comes from concentrated examination of ways in which courses, major programs, and curricular arrangements support and encourage a global dimension. Such a curricular examination will discover areas of strength and practices worth emulating as well as areas of weakness readily capable of improvement. At this juncture in the history of higher education expensive new programs are not going to be attractive to those responsible for the budget. On the other hand, evidence that a college or university has examined and redesigned its offerings with a sense of responsibility to the global dimension should make it attractive to a generation of students who are hungry for the opportunity to understand and to enter this troubled world.

Of course, it is going to take *some* money! At least enough to buy the time of ad hoc faculty committees charged with the mission to do for the world view on their campuses what my college allowed my colleague and me to do for the Negro in American history 20 years ago.

Both from experience and from my sense of the history of American higher education I confess to a profound unhappiness with the notion that great curricular challenges can only be met with great money. That is not the way Greek and Latin moved out of the curriculum nor the way English and economics moved in. On the other hand, alert to our responsibilities to equip our students for the world we foresee rather than the world from which we came, we can do much to facilitate their understanding and to promote their awareness and their skills. To do this we need to scrutinize with imagination and boldness our course syllabi, our appointments and promotions, library acquisitions, the nature of lecture programs, the quality of undergraduate counseling; in short, the whole style of the enterprise. All of this is surely mundane, but it is also where substantive and more permanent curricular change takes place.

Chapter 8

Who Is Tending the Store?

S. Frederick Starr

There is no more broadly accepted gauge of the triumphs and travails of international education programs than the external funds they attract. The slightest hint of a policy shift at any of the major funding agencies will be picked up instantly and transmitted along the nationwide grapevine. Talk of external support is the *lingua franca* of the field, and fluency in that particular language is the surest proof that one is *au courant*.

And for good reason. Because of their peculiar history, international programs at American campuses predominantly owe their origins and—to some extent—their continued vitality to extramural institutions and forces. To be sure, instruction in a few commonly taught foreign languages was long ago established without outside help and is not now dependent on outside subsidies. Most institutions can point also to courses in the literature and history of foreign peoples that enjoy similar independence.

But these are exceptions. International studies entered American higher education because society required them at the moment, and not because the colleges and universities deemed them to be inherently valuable. Throughout the postwar period the chief agents of development and change in international studies have stood outside campus life. Universities have not been entirely passive, to be sure, but they have generally responded to outside stimuli rather than define the necessary changes themselves.

While the inherent provincialism of academia might have contributed to this state of affairs, it is not the only cause of difficulty. On the one hand, the rise of international education coincided with the spread of behaviorism as an organizing principle in the social sciences. Whatever its achievements, behaviorism assigned little importance to the cultural context of human communities, preferring instead to search for the general forces that lie beyond specific cultures. Those social science departments most dedicated to this notion were reluctant to sacrifice positions designated for generalists in order to add foreign area specialists. So much the better, then, if government or foundations would cover the costs.

On the other hand, the thrust toward professionalization in most academic fields made department heads all the more hesitant to dilute their autonomy by encouraging their faculty to participate in the interdisciplinary study that is so much the essence of international education. Only prospects of external support broke this professional and political impasse and made interdepartmental activity acceptable.

It is not necessary to review the immense contributions that outside support has made to the development of international studies. Suffice it to say that between 1951 and 1973 the Ford Foundation alone fed an average of $14 million a year to colleges and universities for this purpose alone, a figure that rose to $27 million annually during the sixties. Other foundations followed Ford's initiatives, while the federal government, through the National Defense Education Act (NDEA), the Fulbright Program, the Peace Corps, and a host of other less publicized measures, added countless millions to the annual total. This is not to deny, of course, that external support in this period also came to play a key role in many other disciplines. But the central importance of such assistance for the broad area of international education was greater than for practically every other field of the humanities and social sciences.

During the 1960s the teaching of international studies was disseminated from the major research universities, where most of the recent PhDs had received their training, to the hundreds of public and private schools that sought to upgrade their offerings in this curricular area. (The extent of this outward decentralization of America's intellectual resources in the international field is worth noting. When the late Ambassador Horace H. Smith catalogued international/intercultural programs at two-year colleges in 1976, he found no fewer than 500 community colleges alone with creditable international programs.)

The only negative side of this achievement is that academics trained during the 1950s and 1960s were used to regarding extramural support as a natural and inevitable part of international education. A generation of professors and graduate students at major research universities simply took it for granted, having known no other system. They carried this attitude with them as they founded new programs elsewhere around the country. Their experience during the flush days of the 1950s and 1960s left them ill prepared to reckon with the straitened budget circumstances occasioned by the post-Vietnam cutbacks. As the smoke cleared, it gradually became apparent how deeply the entire enterprise had been affected. Old bench marks were upturned and new ones became by no means evident.

The situation was confused, but with the benefit of hindsight, one can identify three fundamental conditions that characterized the circumstances of external support for international education during the seventies. All are still operative. First, the relative importance of federal tax dollars as a component of the total of external support has dramatically increased. This increase is perceptible in virtually every phase of academic operations. Where training fellowships formerly came from a number of major foundations, the U.S. Office of Education (now the Department of Education) has become the chief patron, if only by default. In the area of international exchanges, rampant inflation and the changing international position of the dollar made it quite literally impossible for many important programs to survive at all without large federal subventions. Fortunately, they received support, though at the price of conveniently changing their rhetoric from a style that stressed independence from government to a tone that emphasized cooperation with it.

The enlarged role of federal agencies is evident in numerous other areas of international education. Bilingual education, development assistance, scientific cooperation, and programs in such problem areas as agriculture, health, energy, and arms control all reflect the growing share of federal support as a proportion of total support. Recognizing these realities, many universities now maintain regular liaison offices in Washington. Others have filled key staff positions in their international program areas with persons drawn from the Washington bureaucracies. Such backgrounds are now seen as essential for any administrator seeking to make sense of the alphabet soup of federal support programs. Even the august Modern Language Association has followed the dollar by opening a Washington office whence it can monitor programs relevant to its particular mission.

A second aspect of the current situation is that this quasi-governmentalization of international education has been more a consequence of the withdrawal of private support from the field than of any absolute increase in governmental aid. In fact, federal support has eroded at practically every level. The crippling real-dollar cutbacks in the Fulbright Program and in funding for the NDEA are but the best-publicized examples of this development. Compounded through scores of programs in as many agencies, this federal retrenchment has had the effect of rendering federal support less substantial at precisely the moment when dependence upon it has increased.

I can cite as one illustration the fellowships offered by the National Endowment for the Humanities or the Wilson Center, both of which help undergird campus-based activities in the international field. In each case the level of support has so significantly failed to keep abreast of inflation that many senior faculty are unable to accept the terms of appointment without further outside help. But why, one might ask, has support not been concentrated in fewer but larger grants? This has not occurred because the agencies in question must report to congressional committees whose members are drawn from the entire country. Repeated in dozens of agencies, this policy of spreading the money around as widely as possible is having the effect of making each grant less cost effective from the standpoint of both institutional and individual applicants.

Thus the third characteristic of the present situation in federal support is simply this: It has become inconvenient, unreliable, and downright capricious. NDEA applications in all categories demand a far greater investment in institutional time than ever before. But the stakes are lower. Stated differently, it costs more to get less. And few see any realistic prospects of the Office of International Education ever losing its dubious distinction of being the smallest unit within the new Division of Post-Secondary Education of the Department of Education. The dates on which grants are announced have been pushed back, too, so that educational institutions and individual professors do not know until the very last minute whether a given program will be federally funded or needs to be covered by internal funds.

Even these inconveniences would be tolerable if the money pool available for campus programs were at all consistent. But it is not. The National Defense Education Act budget was on a roller coaster for a decade, facing prospects of extinction one year, only to be trebled the next. In March 1980 the U.S. International Communication Agency almost lost $12 million from its exchanges budget for the sole reason that both houses of Congress felt that friends of USICA were less likely than the Federal Trade Commission to mount an effective counterattack against a budget reallocation.

Other federal agencies are thus far holding their own at best. The National Science Foundation, which in its international programs largely deals with international scientific cooperation, has not had a net percentage increase of NSF's total $1 billion budget for some years, nor is this likely. Fellowship programs at the National Endowment for the Humanities were to have had a slight increase in 1981, but this is uncertain as of this writing. Nonetheless, the long-term intent of NEH is to increase its international program dimensions in the years ahead.

Fortunately, federal support does on occasion lurch in more positive directions. In recent months, there was strong Congressional intention to up the new Higher Education Act (Title IV) by $13 million, so as to make possible a range of campus-based programs in international education that "will serve the needs of the business community, including development of new programs for nontraditional, midcareer, or part-time students." It might be added parenthetically that the advisory board being created to oversee this and other international programs is so constituted that only two of its fourteen members are required to have any connection with higher education at all. Even these two posts could be filled by administrators or representatives of national educational organizations, rather than active teachers or scholars.

In a different vein, Representatives Leon Panetta and Paul Simon have put forward individual bills to enhance foreign language learning by students at schools and campuses across the nation. Panetta's bill would provide scholarships for postsecondary majors in language or area studies or other studies requiring significant foreign language learning. Simon's bill would provide "capitation grants" for K-6 and postsecondary students enrolled in certain foreign language courses above some "trigger" level, but excludes support at secondary levels. Whatever their shortcomings, these bills would provide a measure of support that is now absent. There is a strong challenge, however, to the capitation proposal. Educators want support at all levels, in some form other than capitation, and want the wording of the bill to stress language learning integrated with wider international studies.

The ups and downs of federal funds for campus-based programs in international education have often been so sudden and capricious as to make a fool of any academic administrator who fails to hedge his bets. This is not to deny that federal support in various forms is available and of immense importance, given the decline in alternative sources of assistance. But it is already being spread very thin. The process of obtaining it has consequently become more expensive, and the chance of success continues to decline.

It is this combination of circumstances that has impelled a group of major national foundations and corporations to pool their resources in order to launch a National Council on Foreign Language and International Studies. An outgrowth of the recent President's Commission on Foreign Language and International Studies, the council has as its purpose to mount and monitor initiatives in both public and private spheres to improve all aspects of foreign language study and international education in America's schools and universities. A council of elders, with heavy representation from the ranks of industry and public life and with a chairman from the corporate world, the council will inform itself on the needs and concerns of the academic community through a group of advisors and also through liaison with the several regional councils being developed, such as the Bay Area Commission on International Competence (BACIC).

It is risky to predict that any group will succeed in an area in which so many well-intentioned efforts have come to naught. But several factors augur well for the concil's future. First, it will concern itself with both public and private sources of support and be sensitive to the relationship between them. Second, its frank purpose will be to influence the decisions of governmental, corporate, and philanthropic patrons. Its product, in other words, will be concrete actions rather than more resolutions and more reports. Finally, its composition should place it above the clash of factional interests that has often vitiated past efforts to stimulate international studies.

Whatever the fate of this new unofficial coordinating group, the full impact will not be felt for some time. Similarly, the new legislative initiatives are not likely to bear fruit for some while either. In an election year, the drive to balance the budget builds momentum. Authorization is not appropriation, as anyone familiar with the history of the stillborn International Education Act of 1965 will confirm. The newly created HEA Title VI to replace NDEA may only result in more of the same. This means that for the near future academicians will probably be working with approximately the same range of external support sources that exist now. Successful programs will be those that can mobilize these known resources best.

If there is any one fundamental corollary to this overview, it is that the major external sources of support are no longer capable of imparting the permanence and stability to campus programs that they need in order to survive. Whether governmental, philanthropic, or corporate, the external funding bodies today are giving at the margin in order to support their activities that supplement central programs. Their interest lies in buying faculty time to develop experimental training programs or in purchasing scholarly skills for special research assignments. All assume that someone else is taking care of the general maintenance of programs in international studies and foreign languages.

It is well then to ask, who is tending the store? To what extent have universities and colleges succeeded in absorbing the cost of maintaining core programs in international studies and in what ways does that success affect their ability to tap the marginal support that is still available?

Internal institutional support for international programs generally takes three forms. First, it covers the salaries of tenured professors in the relevant departments and generally the salaries of nontenured professors as well. Second, it pays for the maintenance of library collections and personnel. Third, it provides for the use of the institution's physical plant and access to its various support facilities.

As a percentage of total expenditure, these costs can be very high indeed. At NDEA centers they normally constitute between 80 and 90 percent of the total bill. At the vast majority of institutions not receiving support from the Department of Education, the figure is closer to 90 or 95 percent. The implications of this fact are extremely important to the question at hand: For all our talk of the need to mobilize external support for international studies, their day-to-day maintenance is overwhelmingly the responsibility of local institutions. While precise statistics are lacking, the portion of the total bill paid by institutions themselves has certainly risen dramatically during the past decade. Those congressmen and administrators of federal programs who sweep so grandly into the field in order to save international studies would do well to mind those realities. At this point federal programs contribute as much to the problem as they do to the cure. The steadier support of state legislatures, of private institutional endowments, and of tuition-paying students themselves is in fact keeping international programs alive.

Regrettably, national discussion of strong international programs has tended to focus on schools that have depended most heavily on external support. Institutions willing to make the strongest commitment to international programs appear less frequently on lists of grant recipients and hence are less visible to the casual observer. One such program is that of Grinnell College. It has used hardly a penny of federal support in recent years, yet it offers a full range of language courses, as well as area concentrations in European Studies, Latin American Studies, and East European Studies; a new concentration in Asian Studies is now in the planning stage. Crosscutting studies of global issues are also offered. To finance this impressive effort, the board of Grinnell has resolved to raise a special endowment that will eventually cover the salary of a faculty coordinator and various key programmatic expenses.

Yale University is taking a similar tack. Convinced that federal support is likely to be too episodic to assure stability to its programs in the future, Yale's Concilium on International Studies is considering raising a separate endowment of $1 to $3 million. Such a sum would not only cover essential internal operations but would top off the principle accounts for endowed chairs in international studies that have recently been eroded by inflation.

Few schools can afford such an approach, of course, so various substitute strategies are being devised. Undergraduate programs at Pacific Lutheran University, for example, are still heavily dependent on federal support for their maintenance. Up to 40 percent of the $100,000 required each year comes from federal agencies. Yet the plan to internalize the costs is already well advanced, and within five years the entire budget is expected to be picked up by the institution itself.

Some institutions have followed a more adventurous strategy to achieve independence. A solution that is gaining in popularity is that being implemented by the Center for International Studies at the University of North Carolina at Charlotte. Here the principal international activities are carried out by nontenured and adjunct professors. Only about $75,000 of the center's operating budget of $560,000 comes from local (in this case, state) funds, but even this is half again greater than the total federal contribution. The remainder is made up by participant fees and, significantly, by proceeds from a lucrative program in English as a Second Language. By continuing to develop this program, the center's director hopes to achieve still further autonomy.

No absolute level of internal support can, of course, guarantee the security of a program, any more than a given proportion of external funding needs imperil that security. The vital ingredient here is not the amount of internal or external support but the degree to which the institution is willing to act as an insurer of its international programs. At Tulane University, for example, the Center for Latin American Studies receives substantial external support from the federal government, philanthropic and corporate contributors, and regional sources. Nonetheless, Tulane stands firmly behind the center and has committed itself to maintaining essential center functions even in the unlikely event that external support is withdrawn.

The value of such a policy extends well beyond that budget. A recent staff study by the Ford Foundation found that a majority of professors at major centers of international studies were convinced that their programs would cease to exist if government funding were withdrawn. Such an attitude is bound to reduce the willingness of faculty to invest time and professional effort in their institutions, which in turn weakens the case for external support in the first place. The best step university administrators can take to assure outside support for their international programs is to express their backing in the form of an insurance policy.

Whatever strategy is pursued, international programs cannot be permitted to become the victims of uncertainty or caprice at the fed-

eral level. It goes without saying that an institution that possesses secure means, whether from private resources or from a committed state
legislature, enjoys an immense advantage. The key to their development, in turn, is the willingness of an institution's chief administrator
to acknowledge the centrality of international programs and foreign
language study to the life of the school as a whole. But such commitments are not exactly pervasive. All too often the old workplace
adage, "Last on, first off," has been applied to international programs
as well, and with predictable results. Where the commitment is present it is the result either of enlightened administrators or, lacking that,
of successful lobbying within the school by activists in the international field. Indeed, if there is any one absolute requirement both for the
development of internal support and for the mobilization of external
resources, it is the highest possible quality and intensity of faculty
advocacy. Leadership, even more than money, is the very heart of the
matter.

Wherever international programs flourish, one will always find in
evidence strong faculty leadership. This is, of course, a truism that is
also applicable to other fields and disciplines. But the tasks of faculty
leadership in international programs are even broader than in many
other campus activities. Such leadership is necessary to consolidate
the administrative support that is so important in securing outside
backing. High-level initiative is required to elicit the cooperation of
the various departments from which faculty participants in international programs are drawn. Most important, active leadership is necessary in order to take advantage of the innumerable opportunities for
external assistance that are potentially available to international programs even in this period of acute crisis.

A striking historic feature of the field of international education in
the 1960s and early 1970s is the small number of sources upon which
the entire enterprise was built. The number of colleges and universities
involved was then relatively small, and their needs could be met by
the substantial resources made available by a limited number of agencies. By comparison with engineering deans, for example, leaders of
international studies programs had to build contacts with only a modest number of outside agencies in order for their institutions to survive
and flourish. Today all this has changed. Aside from the withdrawal
of the main patrons of a decade ago, international studies can reasonably look to a host of new external sources of funding, information,
and program materials. Those acculturated to academic life in the
heyday of plump Ford grants are perhaps the least likely to explore
these diverse new resources.

My claim that the number of external resources pertinent to international education has increased rather than decreased may require some substantiation. The situation in Russian and Soviet studies may be instructive. In 1975 the American Association for the Advancement of Slavic Studies published a volume entitled *Sources of Support for Training and Research on Russia and the USSR*. It was 61 pages long. In 1979 the Wilson Center's Kennan Institute for Advanced Russian Studies updated that volume. The revised edition runs 140 pages, far longer than can be accounted for by the more thorough editing of the new volume. Were handbooks to be prepared for other world areas and global problems, it is more than likely the results would be similar. Such new sources of support, of course, must be weighed against the evidence of declining support from the major federal programs and private foundations.

Not only has the group of outside agencies providing support and assistance to international programs been expanded, but its character has changed as well. While corporate support for international education is still a minute part of industrial philanthropy—not more than 2 percent of the total—far more companies will entertain proposals in this area than once did. Nor are they all Fortune 500 firms headquartered in New York. As the role of exports in our national economy increases, the willingness of diverse companies to contribute to programs supportive of international economic activity also rises, albeit slowly.

Campus leaders must stay abreast of these developments, especially in their own regions. The development of statewide agencies to promote foreign trade, and the booming international trade marts in New Orleans, Miami, Houston, Seattle, and elsewhere, all attest to the significance of the trend. Nor is language study exempt from this general comment. The fact that private language schools such as Berlitz are flourishing while campus programs languish is indicative of the poor fit between demand and supply in international education. Sophisticated campus programs will want to consider these developments.

A further mission for faculty leadership is to take advantage of the recent entry of foreign governments, foundations, and corporations into the world of educational patronage in the United States. This development has not been without antecedents, such as the establishment of the German Marshall Fund, large gifts by Japanese firms to various American universities, and the efforts by Iran under the Shah to support Middle Eastern studies. The relative decline of the dollar has made such support far more affordable than it was in the past, and the decline in America's world position has caused many friendly governments to explore means of heightening our awareness of the global problems with which the fate of the United States is now so inextricably bound. In some regions, notably in South Carolina, universities have attempted to capitalize on the fact that foreign firms have bought substantial interests in the local economy. Other states have attempted to link support for trade with a given country to the expansion of academic programs for the study of that country. The record of recent gifts, such as Saudi Arabia's grant of $5 million to Princeton for Near Eastern studies, suggests that foreign governments are no more restrictive than our own in specifying the use to which their funds are to be put.

Still another area in which strong campus leadership can make the difference between success and failure is collaborative arrangements among different campuses. Beyond purely intellectual aspects of such cooperation, there are solid practical reasons for pooling resources so as to enable the network to be stronger than any one of its parts. Virtually every component of international studies today is organized into interinstitutional networks, with the field of Soviet studies alone boasting some eight such groups.

A final means by which capable and active leadership can stretch available funds is the establishment of close working ties with the many associations and groups supportive of international studies. The United Nations Association; the Foreign Policy Association; the Society for Inter-Cultural Education, Training, and Research; the Institute for World Order; the Inter-Cultural Associates; the Chicago Council on Foreign Relations; the Southern Center for International Affairs; and other such groups all provide assistance to campus programs.

Leadership is of absolute importance to the success of any programs in international awareness. An institution that invests in its faculty and library but not in its program director will fail to reap the full benefits of its support. In more stable times external resources can be obtained through well-worn channels and used by any faculty member willing to devote the requisite time to the task. Today, because of the rapidly shifting circumstances of federal support, the emergence of new private sources of assistance, the increased role of foreign governments and domestic organizations, and especially the need for international programs to establish a firm base of support within their own institutions, entrepreneurial skills are vital. This, in the last analysis, is the key to the mobilization of external support.

Chapter 9

Toward a Collectivity of Functions

Ralph H. Smuckler

Frederick Starr demonstrates that he is not only *au courant*—in his own use of the term—but also historically well grounded in the ups and downs of external support for international education. He describes clearly and authoritatively the critical importance of outside stimuli to the growth of international education. Starr registers important points, a number of which are not usually dealt with as forthrightly in commentaries on organization and direction of international programs support.

Some of our difficulties in the past, as we urged support for new public policy and encouraged private foundations to fund international education, may have been related to the fact that the field is so ill defined and so pervasive. Indeed, the interests of the actors within it are so varied that they may very well confuse their audiences. In a mix of underfunded and marginally surviving ventures, unproductive rivalries tend to weaken still further the prospects for internationalizing American education.

In my view, the central goal of international education efforts remains what was expressed by the Morrill Committee Report in 1960: the creation of an international *dimension* throughout our academic programs. The dimension takes on different meanings in different disciplines and fields of study. Generally, the international dimension calls for a comparative and Western context. In many fields it also requires a range of knowledge and exposure to non-Western experience. It means that undergraduates, no matter what their field of study, will complete their educational programs with a basic international orientation appropriate to their major field. Beyond this goal of global dimension, international education also encompasses specialized curricula, including area studies, global perspectives, and selected issues. Just as the full range of American higher education contains so much diversity in size, style, and goals, the specific meaning of the international dimension takes on numerous forms from one institution to another. But they share in the ideal of students—both undergraduate and advanced—who are well grounded in the international and comparative context of their studies.

To accomplish such goals, universities can and do draw on a wide range of activities and programs. I would include courses offered in a foreign setting, the education of foreign students and their contribution to the campus environment, area study programs, language learning, problem-oriented international institutes, international development and research activities, faculty exchange programs, long- or short-term cooperative campus programs that yield mutual benefit, and technical assistance projects in which faculty members and graduate students may participate. At a complex university all of these activities may exist; at smaller institutions all may exist on a small scale or some may dominate with the absence of others. The basic point is that there is available a wide range of activities and programs that supply international perspectives.

Professor Starr asks: "Who is tending the store?" He is correct in pointing out that state legislatures, institutional endowments, and tuition-paying students themselves are keeping the programs alive. This broad base is of primary importance, an absolute necessity, especially when viewed against the capriciousness of external support. International studies flourish where those in charge have allocated a good share of institutional resources for those activities. What is then needed, first and foremost, is a significant hold on internal resources and the commitment of those in charge to international dimension goals. Only then would an approach to outside sources of funds be justifiable, mainly for those objectives that cannot be dealt with through institutional resources—i.e., essentially program funds. Such funds can bring vitality to the entire effort. A well-developed institutional program will have identified those items that effectively provide external "mortar" between the bricks provided by internal financing.

The crucial importance of "leadership," singled out by Starr, is worth reemphasizing. I would stress both faculty and academic administrative leadership. The precise pattern varies among our universities, but the need prevails in all. I would add to those the necessity to evolve institutional goals and appropriate strategies. There are many things that can be done by energetic leadership. Helping to fix the course and to put in place the means of evaluating progress stand high among them.

Several years ago a number of us were stressing as an important element of such strategies the need for mutually beneficial long-term international ties that facilitate effective exchange and the sharing of programs. The advantages of such continuing international relationships are many. They include the opportunities to place students with colleagues abroad, to collaborate on research programs, and to set up a regular pattern of exchange. These types of activities, repeated over a number of years, permit faculty members at both ends of such associations to plan sabbatical and other career activities in foreign settings—with some assurance that they will be able to move easily back and forth and accomplish their programs while strengthening the bilateral arrangements. To accomplish such useful institutional ties at the department level or above requires a commitment and a solid base within the campus structure, plus strategic thinking and leadership within the university as a whole. These ties also require outside encouragement and modest but noncapricious funding, which so far have not been forthcoming. The new international program announcements by the National Science Foundation offer some promise, though in a limited sphere. The Institute for Scientific and Technological Cooperation, authorized by Congress but not yet funded, also offers promise.

Leadership is needed to take full advantage of the mutually reinforcing components of numerous international program activities so that they can be put to full advantage. One can certainly strengthen and broaden the contribution of an activity by viewing it within the total institutional approach. Foreign student programs can surely strengthen cocurricular activities which move the campus environment in an international direction. Study abroad programs may fit into the institution's general education requirements; and overseas study may develop around overseas project activity. Area study activities can be strengthened through the buildup of institutional links in the relevant areas, although such ties may have been generated initially by disciplinary or individual efforts. Technical assistance or development research activities may reinforce the quality and opportunities available within a single area study program. All these call for leadership that encourages development of goals plus strategies to achieve them.

The potential for unproductive rivalries within the system—due to prolonged underfunding and the numerous, diverse interests found in the international education universe—is a serious matter. Such disruptive struggles are unacceptable in an era of depleted finances. We need an organization at the national level that speaks for the community of interests with priorities and goals in place. We have not had such a lead point nationally and it is long overdue. My view of the need for better coordination and leadership is based on experience at the university level and at the Washington public and private agency levels.

Stronger processes and sustained leadership nationally would permit a more effective move toward disciplinary and professional associations that have such an important and perhaps crucial impact on university efforts to attain an international dimension. Academic leaders take seriously expression of the values that emanate from accrediting bodies, journals, and disciplinary groups. Such values influence or even dominate the reward system in many campus departments and can be either a positive or a dampening influence. Stronger and more determined leadership nationally could serve to project views in a timely manner and positively influence attitudes within professional and disciplinary associations. We need broad national strategies.

Most of Professor Starr's chapter comes from the viewpoint of a private university. At public institutions funding is generally less flexible, although it may be somewhat more assured. Public institutions tend to experience more difficulty in obtaining international program support from private philanthropy. But they tend to benefit comparatively well from the movement toward public financing, as limited as the total may be. The variety of programs at a public institution is limited by the lower tuition rates. The students may have many different backgrounds, educational and vocational goals, and expectations. The task of educating public governing boards or legislatures to the needs of international directions may be more difficult. But they are equally essential if a more global perspective is to prevail. Public universities, in any event, have tended to carry their public service function into the international arena. They also reflect a basic commitment to citizen education, which has not always been a part of the defined philosophy of private institutions.

Both public and private universities have turned to the federal government for support on scientific exchanges and have been involved in grant and contract activities with the Agency for International Development (AID). In my view the academic benefits accruing to an academic institution through involvement in development assistance research and institution building activities are underplayed in Professor Starr's chapter. The by-product of such efforts ought to be considered seriously as an important source of strength for broader international education purposes. AID supports a range of research activities and institution building activities that can lead to long-term intellectual relationships among faculty members here and abroad. AID-supported activities have been increasingly tied to food, nutrition, and agricultural programs, which has limited but not negated their usefulness as a means of reinforcing broader international programs within American universities.

What do educators have a right to expect from the federal side? In view of government responsibilities to seek successful foreign relations and effective global policies, we should expect at least four things. First, having put our own academic houses in order, we might reasonably expect federal funding for those programs in which a modest federal expenditure would make institutional investments worthwhile. Even small amounts of federal funding can go a long way to stimulate greater institutional investment.

Second, those programs that have proven track records should be placed on a firm base—Fulbright Programs, NDFL fellows, NDEA VI centers, to name a few—so that funding is less capricious. Third, the international research and knowledge building system is sadly and dangerously deficient. The federal government is obligated to strengthen these basic intellectual activities at our universities. Need one cite recent gaps in our expert knowledge and their devastating consequences? What does it take to awaken policy makers to this critical need?

Finally, in international efforts where universities are directly asked to serve national needs, we should expect a system of working together that serves the interests of both government and higher education. Full funding and institutional strengthening activities should be parts of such a system. One would also expect federal assurances of reasonable continuity and evaluative processes that will strengthen, and not weaken, those universities committed to serious international involvement.

Chapter 10

Readings for a Global Curriculum

David J. Dell

While internationalists come to their convictions with considerable passion, a thorough intellectual grounding in the issues remains the more important ingredient. One can only too easily be swayed—indeed, carried away—by the apparent disorder and evangelistic convictions with which many academic internationalists ply their trade. But as global concepts gradually enter the mainstream of educational thought and practice, much of a concrete nature needs to be known about the history, structure, and pedagogic strategies that effective global education inevitably implies.

One might begin one's intellectual journey into the complex world of international education in a myriad of ways. What is suggested here is a mere sampling of important and useful works. They may leave the reader somewhat wiser and, one hopes, better prepared to effect transformations that seem to some of us inevitable.

What kind of knowledge would seem the most essential, and how is this to be applied? That knowledge should include a thorough assessment of the relevant values and limitations inherent in one's own curriculum and an awareness of how the world already impinges on the campus. Books alone cannot supply that knowledge, nor do many faculty or administrators have such knowledge at hand. However, there now exists an extensive literature on foreign language and international studies that is most helpful in educating oneself to the issues at hand.

How the Field Has Developed
One quickly discovers on campuses that international studies and perspectives develop for a great variety of reasons. Changing trends in curricula, new fads and waves in various disciplines, global politics, and powerful issues such as population, peace, poverty, disarmament, and human rights have all left their mark. One also notes that campus responses were in every case achieved through the efforts of dedicated individuals, frequently working alone with little support, often flying in the face of substantial opposition to boot.

One splendid book that combines an overview of the development of foreign area studies with details of the developments on individual campuses is *Internationalizing American Higher Education* by Ellen McDonald Gumperz (University of California, 1970). Tracing the development as far back as 1870 (to make an even 100 years to publication), Gumperz looks at the particulars of programs at 7 colleges and universities (Columbia, Berkeley, Chicago, Mills, Earlham, State University of New York at New Paltz, and the University of Massachusetts at Amherst). In each case, the author notes, local circumstances had a greater impact on the resultant curricula than did national trends, and the influence of catalytic individuals is well documented.

At the same time, however, national efforts provided much of the impetus and justification for introducing and expanding the study of the world in the curricula. Gumperz rightly notes that during the late 1920s and 1930s, several factors combined to produce concerted efforts to get American campuses to teach about the world. Among them were a major international economic crisis, reaction to the Western civilization focus of earlier curricular efforts, and widespread support by intellectuals for international disarmament and for the League of Nations. Champions for the cause were found in the Social Science Research Council, the American Council of Learned Societies (ACLS), and later in the American Council on Education.

The case was made simply and clearly: There were virtually no opportunities for students to learn about other countries and cultures and the study of the international political system remained primitive. The flavor of these times can be gleaned from the *ACLS Bulletin* and from such studies as Symons's *Courses in International Affairs in American Colleges* (Boston: World Peace Foundation, 1932) and Ware's *The Study of International Relations in the United States* (New York: Columbia University, 1934). As W. Norman Brown, who was later to be regarded as the dean of American Indologists, wrote in a 1939 *ACLS Bulletin*:

> Here in the West we still largely confine our humanistic studies to our own civilization. We are concerned with its roots—primitive, prehistoric, and historic—its evolution into its modern state, and the interrelationships of its subdivisions (British, American, French, German, Italian, Russian, etc.). Where the European-Christian culture has clashed with the Far Eastern, the Indic, or the Islamic, we have generally viewed the clash from the point of view of our own narrow prepossessions, with little, if any, comprehension of the reasons the Chinese, the Indians, or the Moslems of Arabia or elsewhere have acted as they have, and without taking a wider world view of these clashes.

That Brown's words of more than 40 years ago should sound so familiar and relevant today is not surprising. The fundamental rationale for international studies carries an enduring validity. A closer look at Brown's essay and the accompanying 200-page survey of Indic resources in the United States by Horace Poleman reveals that there has since been a significant growth in the scale of available resources to meet the continuing need. At the time of Poleman's survey library resources on India in most colleges could scarcely be counted in the tens of books, and courses were astonishingly rare. It would be enlightening for readers to look up their own institutions in the survey and compare the resources available then with what their campuses can mobilize today.

While in the thirties task forces at the ACLS and the Social Science Research Council (with significant foundation support) were laying the groundwork for future growth in area studies programs that focused on specific world cultures, at least one aspect of international studies was by then fairly well established. Within the discipline of political science, courses in international relations and international diplomacy were widely embedded in the field. Norman D. Palmer reviewed the growth of international relations as a field in the fall 1980 issue of *International Studies Quarterly* and cited surveys showing that in the early 1930s fully 3,700 courses in international relations were offered by American colleges. He estimated at least five times that number today. Unlike area studies international relations has secured a firm place within a core academic discipline as one focus of political science. It has grown qualitatively to reflect the use of modern research tools such as computer modeling. In accounting for the growth of the field of international relations over the past 50 years, Palmer noted the seminal leadership of American and European scholars, the increasing complexity and importance of international relations in the "real" world, the growth of the field of political science, and, plainly, a healthy dose of serendipitous expansion.

In addition to area studies and international relations it may be argued that there is a third leg on which the entire enterprise of international studies rests. That is in the area of peace, disarmament, and human rights. The spring 1980 bulletin of the Consortium on Peace Research, Education, and Development includes two articles on the development of cause-related studies in the college curriculum. While firmly founded in values that have been especially welcomed at colleges with religious orientations, such studies have been a vital stimulus to international studies programs across the country.

The legacy of the thirties provided the building blocks for the rapid expansion in international studies following World War II. A generation of scholars with wartime foreign experience and language training received added support with the opening of the Fulbright Program offering a quantum jump in opportunities for research and training abroad. At the same time curricula were opened to non-Western and foreign area studies. With leadership in the humanities from Columbia's Oriental Studies Program, and in the social sciences at the University of Chicago, Berkeley, and elsewhere, as well as strong language requirements in many undergraduate institutions, there was a steady growth of international resources on American campuses. This growth was augmented by increasing international perspectives in such expanding disciplines as anthropology, sociology, and comparative religions. By the time of Sputnik and the independent explosion in enrollments in the sixties the field of international studies was ready for rapid expansion.

Things began to boom for international studies. In the late fifties and early sixties a number of studies were undertaken with support from the Ford Foundation, the Rockefeller Foundation, and the Carnegie Corporation. The National Defense Education Act (1958) promised support for the establishment of centers of excellence to train experts in various languages and foreign areas. The growth in both zeal and numbers is reflected in the sheer volume of publishing on international studies in this prolix period. *Language and Area Studies, A Bibliography* (New York: Foreign Area Materials Center, 1966) lists nearly 500 books and articles, including 45 titles pertaining exclusively to undergraduates. Among many worth citing are Percy Bidwell, *Undergraduate Education in Foreign Affairs* (New York: Kings Crown, 1962), Howard E. Wilson and Florence F. Wilson, *American Higher Education and World Affairs* (Washington, D.C.: American Council on Education, 1963), and Milton Singer, et al., "Chicago's Non-Western Civilization Program" (*Journal of General Education*, January 1959).

Overnight the entire field of international studies was transformed from a continuing uphill struggle to flat-out acceleration. Annual PhD production doubled and then doubled again. Area studies centers were established at many universities, interdisciplinary programs were established almost at will in college curricula, and it seemed that international studies would continue to grow almost indefinitely. The exponential growth is illustrated in the increase in numbers of extracurricular programs surveyed in *The International Programs of American Universities* (published jointly by the East-West Center and Michigan State University, First Edition 1958, Second Edition 1966). Over the brief span between the two editions, the number of programs listed burgeoned from 382 to over 1,300. The concise program descriptions remain valuable as a survey of what can be done at institutions of all sizes and types in establishing programs outside the curriculum.

By the end of the sixties the boom in international studies had run its course and the first signs of retrenchment appeared, though they were still apparent only to a few. Federal support was waning, and while thousands of PhDs with international competence had been placed in institutions across the country, the number of new positions began to decline. Courses that had been designed to fit core curricular needs dropped in enrollment when the general relaxation of curricular requisites pushed toward removing all requirements from the curriculum (especially languages). Conversely, interdisciplinary programs without firm footholds in departments became more susceptible to budget cutbacks. The shift of student interests from international idealism in the early sixties to activism against the war in Vietnam in the late sixties did not hurt the field. But the subsequent reaction against American international involvement of *any* kind, combined with the increased career orientation of undergraduates, did contribute to the end of the expansion. Possibly international studies did not suffer out of proportion to other fields of study. But in contrast to its earlier growth, the fall seemed particularly spectacular. The perception of the field, at least, was that an era had ended, perhaps never to return. The mood generally changed from heady expansionism to that of grim survival.

Much of the literature on international studies of the seventies reflects that change. There is a general focus on the quality of programs and personnel, on identifying workable roles for international studies that will strengthen curricula rather than simply add to them. One work of the early seventies deserves special attention: Richard Lambert's *Language and Area Studies Review* (Philadelphia: American Academy of Political and Social Science, 1973). Lambert's call for developing the educational roles of established centers, for integrating and rationalizing existing programs, and especially for improving the competence (especially in languages) of area studies specialists already in teaching positions continues to have relevance.

Another valuable resource is the International Education Project of the American Council on Education, first underwritten by the Ford Foundation; it serves as an information clearinghouse and voice for the field. As director of the project over much of this period, Rose Lee Hayden was called upon to advocate increased support and urge the field of international studies to get its own act together. Among her numerous speeches and essays, often cited is her statement before the

Senate Appropriations Subcommittee on Labor/Department of Health, Education, and Welfare, September 21, 1977. It is a cogent statement of the need and rationale for foreign language and international studies in the context of U.S. priorities. A lengthier statement worth consulting is Robert E. Ward's *National Needs for International Education* (Washington, D.C.: Center for Strategic and International Studies, Georgetown University, 1977).

While the seventies were a period of retrenchment and reassessment for international studies, a number of factors outside the field began to generate a general resurgence. New crises awaited the U.S. after Vietnam. The rise of OPEC, Cuban troops in Angola, the Panama Canal Treaty, and other issues demanded an informed policy debate. The need for campus-based expertise was underlined, among others, when it was revealed that only a handful of American scholars on Africa had ever been to Angola. Proponents of international causes regrouped after Vietnam and human rights began to receive special attention, first in reference to Chile and South Africa, and later on globally. The SALT talks and the Helsinki accords added topicality to issues of peace and disarmament. They received added emphasis with the 1976 Presidential campaign and with the election of Jimmy Carter on a platform that emphasized human rights and disarmament. Energy, the decline in the value of the dollar, and events in Iran added further momentum.

When the Ford Foundation convened a meeting of the presidents of 15 major universities in early 1978 to address the needs of academic competence in world areas, and the new Harvard curriculum gave emphasis to non-Western studies (both events generating wide publicity), luster was added to the general thrust of international studies.

These forces were harnessed to set in motion a new round of studies on the field (including the Council on Learning project, Education and the World View), which have begun to appear in the past year. Together they amount to a fairly complete reassessment of foreign language and international studies. The combined weight of these studies is expected to augur well for increased federal and private support focused largely on higher education programs.

International Studies Today
On September 15, 1978, President Carter appointed the President's Commission on Foreign Language and International Studies. A year later, following extensive fact finding, input from the field, and attendant publicity, the work of the commission was completed and published as *Strength Through Wisdom, A Critique of U.S. Capability: A*

Report to the President from the President's Commission on Foreign Language and International Studies, U.S. Department of Health, Education, and Welfare, November 1979. U.S. Government Printing Office #017-080-02065-3 (for typeset version: the American Council on Teaching of Foreign Languages, 2 Park Ave., New York, N.Y. 10016).

The establishment of a President's commission was a major event in the field, as it focused public attention and solicited comments from a cross-section of the combined fields of foreign language and international studies. While the report itself contains extensive recommendations for federal government support of the field, it also provides an approximate consensus of what the overall state of the field is and should be. Special attention to college and university programs is given in chapter III, where, among other prescriptions, it is recommended that: "With the possible exception of some so-called pure sciences, international and comparative perspectives should be part of the teaching of most subjects. To this end colleges and universities should encourage their faculty members to use sabbaticals and other professional growth opportunities to strengthen their international skills and experience."

More in-depth attention to the needs of colleges can be found in the accompanying volume, *President's Commission on Foreign Language and International Studies: Background Papers and Studies*. Of special interest here is James Harf's "Undergraduate International Studies: The State of the Art and Prescriptions for the Future" (pp. 90-103). Using formal responses from over 200 colleges and universities, the author stresses the broadest possible integration of international studies into the undergraduate curriculum in order to attack the "97 percent rate of complete noninvolvement in any international experience by the student body."

The President's commission was very much in public view during its year of fact finding and open hearings. Thus it necessarily reflects the perceived self-interests of the major constituencies of the field and tends to legitimate those interests. Its value is enhanced rather than diminished when used in conjunction with other recent studies that enjoyed the leisure and privacy needed for a more critical assessment. Performing this role in the area of foreign language teaching is *Language Study for the 1980's: Reports of the MLA-ACLS Language Task Forces*, Richard I. Brod, ed. New York: Modern Language Association, 1980. 106 pp.

Based on a series of five task force reports commencing in 1976 and completed in 1979, this volume is remarkable on two counts: It includes clearly written and cogent recommendations and it does not hesitate to direct a large portion of those to language teachers. Of special interest to the college administrator will be the first section ("Report of the Task Force on Institutional Language Policy," pp. 8-18). These pages condense 52 recommendations into three main subject headings: Language Programs in Education and Society, Language Programs Within the Institutional Context, and Mechanisms for Effecting Change. Among the recommendations are active involvement of language faculty in general education; developing courses away from the traditional literary focus of advanced language training; scheduling and devising courses that lead to fulfillment of a proficiency requirement rather than semester hours; and establishment of modes for greater cooperation on curriculum among language departments within an institution. Overall the volume aims at a comprehensive agenda for improving language study in the coming decade and is a valuable starting point for anyone seeking to design or legitimate changes in language teaching.

Two recent studies commissioned by the Ford Foundation—and available from the foundation—give special attention to the future of international studies with reference to conditions prevailing in major research-oriented universities. *International Studies Review: A Staff Study* by Elinor G. Barber and Warren Ilchman reports on a survey jointly undertaken by the foundation and the National Endowment for the Humanities at 15 major universities. The survey was intended to assess the probable output and placement opportunities in terms of PhD candidates, ascertain the strength and likely continuance of existing programs (including maintaining faculty lines), and identify needs in relation to available external support for research and facilities. While the study focuses on the situation of major research institutions, it contains considerable information useful to any program, especially since all of the universities surveyed were sensitive to the needs of the undergraduate curriculum. The chapter "Factors in the General Vitality of International Studies" makes for salutary reading at all levels of higher education. A second report to the Ford Foundation, *The Permanent Revolution: An Assessment of the Current State of International Studies in American Universities*, by Robert A. McCaughey, provides a critical review of the frequent cries of international studies faculties that they suffer especially during these penurious times. In his view, "International studies academics could help themselves by engaging somewhat more in the kinds of curricular planning—and curricular politicking—that other academics, lacking the outside funding and release-time-from-teaching benefits they enjoyed until recently, have always regarded as a necessary part of their professional lives."

McCaughey argues that, through dispersion of international studies talent into the four-year and two-year colleges, international studies has now secured a permanent place in the American curriculum.

Barbara B. Burn had already begun a comprehensive review of international studies when she was called upon to serve as the executive director of the recent President's commission. Her book, *Expanding the International Dimension of Higher Education* (San Francisco: Jossey-Bass, 1980), which was prepared for the Carnegie Council on Policy Studies in Higher Education, provides a sound general introduction to the field, in the context of social and educational developments and in reference to developments in international education at the undergraduate level. The book is especially valuable for information about what various organizations and funding agencies in the field have been attempting in recent years. The concluding chapter, "Organizing for International Education," addresses the problems and potential for attaining harmonious cooperation in this diffuse and complex field, an area where the author has had much professional experience.

While each of the above studies is deserving of praise in its own right, the May 1980 issue of the *Annals of the American Academy of Political and Social Sciences: New Directions in International Education*, edited by Richard D. Lambert, serves as a commentary on all. It provides the missing ingredients to make them a comprehensive critical assessment of the field. The concluding essay by Lambert, "International Studies: An Overview and an Agenda," provides a number of thoughtful insights and focuses directly on the need of the field to actively participate in general education. His words bear repeating:

> If we really want to make a dent upon the outlook of a substantial number of our students, we will have to reach more of them, and this means adding an international component to a large number of courses, including those that are currently entirely domestic in their subject matter. This approach has two prerequisites: an institutional will to accomplish it, one shared by faculty and students, and a faculty with enough international competence to be able to provide professional-level instruction.

Toward Implementation
Armed with knowledge of local circumstances and an overview of international studies, one may well wish to persevere and develop an improved foreign language and international studies capability on one's own campus. The underlying premise of this volume of Change Magazine Press and of the broad-based Council on Learning's Education and the World View project, is to provide successful and replic-

able examples of how other institutions have undertaken this task. There are, in addition, a number of published descriptions of programs both within and beyond the curricula that can provide how-to knowledge and spare enthusiasts the burden of reinventing the wheel. Indeed, the Council has now published its own compilation of 50 workable international programs.

Much of the programming skill in international studies resides in fact in the memories of individuals on scattered campuses. These have never been collated. Some such program descriptions surface as brief conference reports or articles in assorted journals, usually not widely read. Consequently there is no single national source for guidance. Perhaps the best single source of ideas on internationalizing curricula in the undergraduate environment remains unpublished. In the past decade the Department of Education's Office of International Programs has funded hundreds of undergraduate programs, and the proposals of funded applicants remain on file as a matter of public record. Whether seeking funding or not, anyone contemplating organizing the presence of the world on his campus should invest the time to visit, browse through these proposals, and consult with the Washington staff.

On a more modest scale, examples of attempts to remodel curricula in the 1970s can be found in *International/Intercultural Education in the Four Year College: A Handbook on Strategies for Change* by Marvin Williamsen and Cynthia Morehouse (New York: Learning Resources in International Studies, 1977). Based on a Wingspread conference in 1975, the handbook addresses both institutional development (with examples from Florida's Eckerd College, Ramapo College of New Jersey, and Michigan State) and faculty development (focusing on practices at Davidson College, the Great Lakes Colleges Association, and the State University of New York). In addition to concrete examples the book provides a valuable checklist of "successful contributing factors" and a section on the theory and practice of instructional development. It is available from Learning Resources in International Studies, 60 East 42nd Street, New York, N.Y. 10165.

Also worth consulting are *International/Intercultural Education in Selected State Colleges and Universities: An Overview and Five Cases* by Audrey Ward Gray (Washington, D.C.: American Association of State Colleges and Universities, 1977) and *Internationalizing Community Colleges* edited by Roger Yarrington (Washington, D.C.: American Association of Community and Junior Colleges, 1978), which provide case studies of various programs in their respective types of institutions.

Beyond the Curriculum

Creating a global curriculum in itself is a worthwhile endeavor, but most successful programs involve matters well beyond curricular issues. Two noncurricular areas deserve attention: utilization of the community and study abroad.

1. Utilizing the Community

In assessing and organizing resources for a globalized curriculum, it is foolish to overlook the fact that there exists a substantial external resource base (and, incidentally, a significant market) surrounding almost any campus. Few realize the extent to which nearly every American community has gone international. Ethnic heritage and tourism abroad are just the tip of the iceberg. Churches, YMCAs, Rotaries, even hospitals as well as other civic organizations have become prime focuses of international experience and activity. Export, import, banking—commerce of all kinds—generates international awareness on the part of local residents, not to mention the attraction of foreign visitors.

Pioneering work in looking at the extent of international resources and interaction in the community has been done during the past decade at the Mershon Center of Ohio State University. Under the leadership of Chadwick Alger (a past president of the International Studies Association), and with funding from the Kettering Foundation and others, the Mershon Center set out to analyze and develop community resources in the city of Columbus. It has been published in a Mershon Center series: *Columbus in the World, The World in Columbus.* This and other studies can revolutionize one's thinking about the parochial nature of heartland America. Recently this project has produced a handbook for anyone who wishes to conduct a similar exercise in his or her own community. *You and Your Community and the World* by Chadwick F. Alger and David G. Hoopler (New York: Learning Resources in International Studies, 1979) is designed for the independent user; or it can form the basis of a course in community sociology.

2. Study Abroad

Most campuses, large and small, have, or have access to, organized study abroad programs. Many colleges have built upon their study abroad programs by integrating them with language and international study. They often offer a distinctive attraction for potential applicants. A review of the literature will quickly reveal that no two programs are alike, even when they are run by the same college in the same country. On the other hand, there are now hundreds of programs available where students from any number of colleges come together in a program run by a single institution or a consortium. Whether one plans to build study abroad programs on one's own campus or capitalize on the opportunities for sharing programs, there is a considerable literature available offering sound theoretical and practical advice.

The three primary sources of information are the Council on International Educational Exchange (CIEE), the Institute on International Education (IIE), and the National Association for Foreign Student Affairs (NAFSA). CIEE is a membership organization providing services and information to 182 member colleges and educational institutions. It focuses on travel services and offers charter flights, travel insurance, work/study abroad opportunities, hostels, evaluation of programs, and other aids in addition to its publications. It also publishes *The Whole World Handbook* (New York: an Arthur Frommer publication, distributed by Simon & Schuster, Sixth Edition, 1978). The book describes the conditions students are likely to find in the countries they visit and gives synopses of programs sponsored in each country by CIEE members.

Publications of the National Association for Foreign Student Affairs, including the NAFSA newsletter published nine times yearly, contain numerous suggestions for developing and improving study abroad programs. Of special interest is Ivan Putman's *Study Abroad: A Handbook for Advisers and Administrators* (Washington, D.C.: NAFSA, 1979), which provides the essential information needed to establish and manage a program, including rationales for programs, the advisory process, and tips on administration. *Study Abroad Programs: An Evaluation Guide* (Washington, D.C.: NAFSA, 1979) discusses criteria for evaluating programs and includes Xeroxable questionnaires for participants, alumni, administrators, and on-site evaluators.

The Institute on International Education in New York carries an extensive list of publications, including *Grants for Study Abroad* (cited below), as well as joint publications with the Council on International Educational Exchange.

Generating External Support

In the current decline of educational resources, the ability to attract outside support often makes the crucial difference in the survival of nontraditional programs. The multifaceted nature of international studies, coupled with the continuing interest of key supporters, makes international studies eligible for a bewildering array of types and

sources of support. What outside financial support lacks in overall
dollar amounts it makes up in diversity. There simply exists such an
array of programs offering direct support for campus programs, opportunities for faculty research and exchange abroad, and support for
visiting scholars that virtually every campus can expect to be eligible
for a number of grants, most of them modest, and other forms of assistance.

In a recent study it was estimated that as much as 15 percent of all
program support for international studies comes from extrainstitu-
tional sources, including a number of federal agencies, foreign governments, foundations, and corporate donors. No program can long en-
dure on soft money alone, of course. For most, the development of effective entrepreneurial acumen can take several years before outside
funding can become a significant factor in cost support. The *CISP International Studies Funding Book* (New York, Council for Intercultural Studies and Programs, Second Revised Edition, 1980) describes
some 250 grant programs available to individuals and institutions. It
supplies the addresses for over 150 U.S.-based organizations offering
various types of informational resources and 100 contact points in foreign governments where further opportunities may be found. The
book includes a solid bibliography of information on funding and program development, a concise listing of useful newsletters, summaries
of past conferences on funding international studies, and profiles of 18
U.S. cultural institutions that provide significant support for international studies.

A number of other sources of information are available, including
the Association of American Colleges Federal Resources Advisory
Service (1818 R Street, N.W., Washington, D.C. 20036); the Institute
for International Education's *Grants for Study Abroad 1980* (809
United Nations Plaza, New York, N.Y. 10017) and other related texts;
and the International Studies Association's *Grants and Fellowships in
International Studies* (c/o Department of Government and International Studies, University of South Carolina, Columbia, S.C. 29208).

Readings for the Future
Today's timely information soon enough turns into history. Any vigorous international program office needs multiple sources of continuing information to keep abreast of new developments and opportunities. Many such sources already cross different faculty desks on every
campus, but few faculty or administrators see more than a few of
them. Members of each area studies association receive quarterly
newsletters, but there is little overlap in membership. Similarly, bulle-

tins in the humanistic disciplines and the Association of Departments of Foreign Languages bulletin contain information of use beyond their own membership.

Within the field of international studies a number of periodicals have stood the test of time and should be consulted as soon as they appear for announcements of conferences, new publications and programs, and funding opportunities. The following newsletters are especially useful: *ISIS* (Intercultural Studies Information Service), published by the Council for Intercultural Studies and Programs, 60 East 42nd Street, New York, N.Y. 10165. *IIE Reports*, published by the Institute for International Education, 809 United Nations Plaza, New York, N.Y. 10017. *ICIP Newsletter*, published by the Indiana Consortium for International Programs, Indiana University at Kokomo, Kokomo, Ind. 46901. *American Association of State Colleges and Universities Newsletter*, published by the American Association of State Colleges and Universities, One Dupont Circle, N.W., Washington, D.C. 20036. *NAFSA Newsletter*, published by the National Association for Foreign Student Affairs, 1860 19th Street, N.W., Washington, D.C. 20009.

This, then, constitutes somewhat of a crash reading course on some crucial elements of international education. It is neither the beginning nor the end of a fuller comprehension of the necessary restructuring of a college education that can keep pace with a world that, unhappily, was not invented on the nation's campuses. Alas, global realities do not compartmentalize themselves into the neat cubbyholes of the disciplines. For the academic professional, a fuller immersion in the bouillabaisse of international curricular issues makes for untidy prospects. Nonetheless, that immersion has become a matter of moment far transcending the in-house faculty debates over business-as-usual.

1981 Publications in the Education and the World View Series

The Role of the Scholarly Disciplines

This book focuses on the potential role of the disciplines in encouraging enlarged international dimensions in the undergraduate curriculum; it also provides useful insights into campus initiatives and effective curricular approaches. **$4.95**

The World in the Curriculum: Curricular Strategies for the 21st Century

Written by Humphrey Tonkin of the University of Pennsylvania, this volume considers concrete, feasible recommendations for strengthening the international perspective of the undergraduate curriculum at academic institutions; it provides a guide to meaningful curricular change for top administrators and faculty. **$6.95**

Education for a Global Century: Issues and Some Solutions

A reference handbook for faculty and administrators who wish to start or strengthen language and international programs, this contains descriptions of exemplary programs, definitions of minimal competencies in students' international awareness and knowledge, and recommendations of the project's national task force. **$7.95**

Education and the World View

A book edition of Change's special issue on Education and the World View for use by trustees, faculty, and administrators; it also contains proceedings of a national conference that considered the implications of educational ethnocentrism and action to encourage change. **$6.95**

What College Students Know About Their World

An important new national assessment of American freshmen and seniors, conducted by the Educational Testing Service, that covers the strengths and weaknesses of American college students' global understanding; an aid to faculty and program directors, it pinpoints areas for improving international content. **$5.95**

Education and the World View Conference/Workshop Kit

A comprehensive kit to assist faculty and institution and program administrators in providing focused debate and planning on curricular change to strengthen international dimensions at their institutions, either independently or with Council on Learning guidance. **$14.95**

For further information about these Council on Learning publications, write Change Magazine Press, 271 North Ave., New Rochelle, N.Y. 10801.